In a world of hustle and pressure to do all the things, needed guide to put comparison aside and instead pose, patience, and intention.

—**Jordan Lee Dooley**, *Wall Street Journal* bestselling author of *Own Your Everyday*

If you have ever thought, "I have a dream, but I don't know where to start," this is the book for you! Dreams don't just come true without the dreamer putting in the work. In this book, Jenny encourages you to take small steps daily to work toward your goal, and she continually points you to the truth about who you are because of God's love for you. This is the gospel-centered "you can do it" book we've been looking for!

—**Jamie Ivey**, bestselling author and host of
*The Happy Hour with Jamie Ivey* podcast and *The Jamie Ivey Show*

I absolutely *love* how Jenny doesn't allow us to language-labor over dreams we've put on a shelf. Instead, every chapter of *Dream Come True* is filled with practical and logical steps that will help you dust off the delusions and see your dream come true! Jenny offers the creative coaching you need to step outside your fantasy and walk confidently with your greatest visions into reality. Beautifully written and designed, *Dream Come True* will become a page-turner to read and a scrapbook to hold the memories of the moment your "maybe someday" turned into "today."

—**Candace Payne**, viral sensation + joy evangelist

*Dream Come True* takes the dream that feels impossible and abstract and makes it approachable, clear, and achievable. Jenny has a gift to help people not only to dream but also to see those dreams turn into reality. As we move into what God is calling us to do and be, we all need partners, advocates, and friends, and Jenny will be that person for you. In these pages, you'll find yourself looking upward to God, working inward to the heart, and moving forward to understand the dream God has put in you. Your dream doesn't have to remain a dream—this book will help you make your dream come true.

—**Mark Schilling**, pastor, Redeemer Church, Rome, New York

Jenny Randle does it again with *Dream Come True*. Her incredible ability to apply Scriptural truth to your personal journey and goals is life changing. Her book offers a practical guide to dreaming with God about your destiny and taking practical steps to reach those goals. Her creativity is unparalleled by anyone I know. After reading *Dream Come True*, you will sense a renewed passion for your purpose. This Christ-centered book is a hands-on guide with one power punch after another. Get your copy and get ready to not only dream but also make that dream a reality!

—**Brynn Shamp**, cofounder and CEO of Destiny Encounters International

# *Dream*
# COME
# TRUE

## JENNY RANDLE

HARVEST HOUSE PUBLISHERS
EUGENE, OREGON

Cover design by Studio Gearbox

Cover photo © Midstream / Shutterstock

Interior design by Janelle Coury

# Dream COME TRUE

Copyright © 2021 by Jenny Randle
Published by Harvest House Publishers
Eugene, Oregon 97408
www.harvesthousepublishers.com

ISBN 978-0-7369-8119-4 (pbk.)
ISBN 978-0-7369-8120-0 (eBook)

Library of Congress Cataloging-in-Publication Data

Names: Randle, Jenny, author.
Title: Dream come true / Jenny Randle.
Description: Eugene, Oregon : Harvest House Publishers, [2021] | Includes
   bibliographical references.
Identifiers: LCCN 2021018603 (print) | LCCN 2021018604 (ebook) | ISBN
   9780736981194 (pbk.) | ISBN 9780736981200 (ebook)
Subjects: LCSH: Vocation—Christianity. | Dreams—Religious
   aspects—Christianity. | Self-actualization (Psychology)—Religious
   aspects—Christianity. | Procrastination—Religious
   aspects—Christianity. | BISAC: RELIGION / Christian Living / Devotional
   | RELIGION / Christian Living / Calling & Vocation
Classification: LCC BV4740 .R36 2021  (print) | LCC BV4740  (ebook) | DDC
   248.4—dc23
LC record available at https://lccn.loc.gov/2021018603
LC ebook record available at https://lccn.loc.gov/2021018604

**Printed in the United States of America**

21 22 23 24 25 26 27 28 29 / VP-JC / 10 9 8 7 6 5 4 3 2 1

To my children, Max and Zoey
*You have a purpose. You are bold. You are loved.*

And to the action takers, dreamers, and moment makers
*It's not about what or how much you do but Whom you do it for.*

*It's time to answer the call.*

# Contents

*After you complete each Next Best Adventure Step.*
*check it off here.*

## ACT 1: THE DIVINE STRATEGIC PLAN

## ACT 2: NIGHTMARE EXCUSES OR PEACEFUL ASSURANCE

# A NOTE FROM JENNY

To the recovering procrastinators,

*I see you.* I played "hard to get" with a dream for ten years. As a professional creative, I found myself living in a performance-mentality zone, riddled with anxiety and comparing myself to everyone. A secret dream was on my heart, but I continually ignored it because "Why would I do that?"

Everything changed as Jesus got ahold of my heart, broke the chains of inadequacy and fear, and taught me about His truth and my identity in Him. He gave me the strength to take one small step toward the dream, and I haven't stopped since. In this space of freedom, God has empowered me to help others take action and live on purpose.

I know dreams and goals change with the seasons. The occupational dream I had as a third grader carried me into my twenties. Then God began to speak a new goal that is taking me into my forties. I also had additional dreams, like producing a TV show, having a family, and learning to understand Sabbath rest. I believe God is awakening a dream or two for you too. Pick a goal (any size will do) and tackle it throughout the pages of this book. If you're unsure what that goal might be, I pray God will use these words to awaken a new dream for you!

Your calling from God may look and sound different from other people's because God wired you with unique talents and abilities. Let me show you what I mean. A few months ago, my parents and I were chatting around the table at their house. My little bro was there, who, as it turns out, isn't so little anymore. He's a good-guy lawyer who married an amazing, kind, smart woman we call "the good doctor." For obvious reasons, I've nicknamed lawyer bro and neurologist sis-in-law "the power couple." I realize they are more than their job titles and duties, but I'm proud of them, so let it be.

Since the power couple was right in front of me, I asked them a pressing question about an issue a close friend was having with an elderly relative. My brother launched into the need for a power of attorney and living trust. Then the good doctor described the signs and symptoms of dementia. As I struggled to decipher the legalese and medical jargon, I made a self-deprecating joke. My mom then "mommed" the moment and said, "You're all smart in different ways."

A few months later, the power couple called me for advice on how to help a colleague find a book publisher. After asking me to re-explain some of my advice, Bro sheepishly added, "We're all smart in different ways." This statement has now become the family joke when we need each other's support. And now you're in on the joke too because we all need that mom reminder every now and then, don't you think? *We're all smart in different ways!*

If there's one thing to remember as you work through God's dream for you, it's this: Comparison will crush your calling. Yes, we can look to some people as examples in the faith or as models of how to get it done. But don't compare yourself to them, because you don't know the whole story. God is working in and through their lives just as He is in and through yours. In fact, this whole thing is His story anyway.

*Dream Come True* isn't a frivolous, feel-good motivator for you to find your inner strength as you live the American dream. The hope is that you will live God's dream as you find your strength in Christ. Faith-filled dreams come alive with action. God is actively inviting you to come to Him with those unique smarts of yours and obediently pursue His will for your life.

Let it shine—you're designed for this!

*Jenny Randle*

# Lord.

May Your dreams become mine. I don't ever want to dream to gain status or to feel significant. I'm sorry for the times I dove into selfish or shallow ambition outside Your will. Help me to follow You more and pursue my plans less. I want to dream because I'm beginning to hear You inviting me to stand in holy places. In these places, You transform buried potential into beautiful possibilities.

*Equip* me for the BIG dreams that others
reject because they feel intimating.

*Embolden* my spirit.

*Equip* me for the smaller dreams that I often
reject because they feel insignificant.

*Embolden* my spirit.

*Help* me to steward my life honorably, and
teach me how to live on purpose.

I believe You are an all-knowing, all-powerful God who will empower me to step boldly into areas I have yet to recognize. I dream because You're a God who brings redemption to the broken, paints the darkness with light, and breathes life into my lungs. I know that You have yet to say "Well done." How can I commune with You and not contend for the things You've invited me to? As Your dreams flood my mind, will You help me to fully embrace them in my heart?

Above all else, may I trust You. Turn my acts of obedience into acts of worship because You're worthy. I dream, not to be seen but to see You more clearly. Use me for Your glory and for the good of others. Help me to give You all the praise.

In Jesus's name,

*amen.*

# WHAT IS *DREAM COME TRUE*?

*Dream Come True* is like a guidebook to help you pursue God's calling in your present circumstances. If you don't have a dream right now, don't worry! Maybe God is inviting you to encourage someone else in theirs. This resource offers a proven framework for reaching your goal or aspiration by eliminating excuses and procrastination and taking action!

You'll learn about Moses. God gave him a huge assignment—to liberate the Israelites—but he protested and felt unqualified for the call. Applying his play-by-play to your own experience is like looking at your Aunt Mary's journey to becoming a Broadway superstar. Just hearing of God's faithfulness will propel you forward. You'll gain wisdom from godly leaders who went before us, and you'll learn from some recovering procrastinators who were sleeping on the job.

This book will help you answer the question "What do I do next?" You'll discover what a kingdom mindset is and be empowered to maintain that way of thinking. You'll also work through your personalized Divine Strategic Plan on pages 47-49. Most importantly, you will see the big picture of God's story and find your place in it. Are you ready to realize what it looks like to rest in Christ while representing Him? Wake up, dreamer—God is calling you!

## Things You'll Need

computer or smartphone       Bible       journal

pen or pencil       colored pencils       awesomeness

willingness to commit       a spirit to do hard things

## Guidelines for Your Dream to Come True

1. This book includes a short lesson, question, or action step and prayer each day. Check off the box on the contents page after you complete each chapter.

2. At the end of every lesson, you can continue to the next chapter, or you can create your own path based on how you feel God is directing you. Both journeys provide forward momentum toward completion as you take your Next Best Adventure Step.

3. This is a 31-day interactive experience. The book has room for you to doodle, write notes, and highlight text. There are reflective questions, tasks and tools, and empty spaces to get messy.

4. Do the work. This works well when you are actively working toward a goal. If you don't have a goal, let's pray God will uncover one for you in the process.

5. Listen for God's voice as you plan your next best steps, and remind yourself often that He's the author of your story and is inviting you to be a part of it.

6. Have fun! The chapters will keep you from falling into performance mode or feeling overwhelmed. Develop a healthy mindset as you take your next step into the things God is doing.

7. Invite a friend on this journey with you, and use #dreamcometruebook so we can get social and cheer you on in your journey. Everything is better with friends!

## Commitment Contract

There's power in community. Text or call a trusted friend and ask him or her to hold you accountable to finish this book. Better yet, buy the person a copy and do it together!

I, _____, commit to pursuing God's will for my life in this right-now season. I will follow God's leading as this dream comes true. I'm ready to get uncomfortable, show up, and do the hard stuff. I'm trusting God to work in and through me throughout this process. May I glorify and honor Him as I do.

My accountability partner is _____.
This person committed to encouraging me to do hard things.

_____          _____
*your signature*                                              *date*

_____          _____
*accountability partner signature*                     *date*

# GOD LEADS US BY ESTABLISHING DIRECTION AND CALLING US TOWARD HIM.

# Act 1

## The Divine Strategic Plan

# 1

# INTRODUCTION TO ACT 1

*We are not called to be safe, we are simply promised
that when we are in danger, God is right there with us.
And there is no better place to be than in His hands.*

KATIE J. DAVIS

Imagine this: You and I are training together, similar to that iconic scene from the movie *Rocky*. The theme song is blaring as we run around town in a really long montage of us flipping tires, boxing, and pretending the floor is lava. Kids and unicorns are running behind us because we're freakin' legends (or so we think). You're wearing a two-piece gray tracksuit, and I'm in my elephant jammies because...well, it just seems right. The music peaks as we sprint-stumble up the steps of that fancy building. Time slows, we face one another, and...*you're now mentally pumped to embrace what I'm about to say.*

God is not writing a boring, unadventurous story for your life. On the other hand, he doesn't want you to awkwardly strive to win people's praise. We live somewhere between grit and grace, learning how to live with purpose in our careers, side hustles, and callings. From the time humanity fell into sinful rebellion by ignoring God's voice, our work has been a struggle (Genesis 3:17-19). The great news of the gospel is that Christ redeems the broken things.

Your adventurous life isn't a storybook quest to slay dragons or to achieve fist-pumping triumphs; it's a real battle against the enemy of your soul as you learn to embrace the victory that Christ already won. Are you ready to train up and run with endurance, eyes fixed forward on Jesus? Even in our moments of monotony or deep suffering, God speaks, awakening adventure as we follow Him toward a life of freedom, purpose, and bravery.

## IT'S NOT TIME TO SHRINK BACK; IT'S TIME TO SHOW UP!

## How Answering the Call Causes Action

Have you ever gotten a phone call that radically changed everything for the better?

☐ Nah, who answers the phone these days?
(Turn to the dedication page.)

☐ Yes, I'm so glad I picked up!

Maybe it was an employer offering you a new job or a doctor telling you the cancer is in remission. Was it a call from your bestie, celebrating because she was accepted at the same college you attend? Or a foster-care agency requesting to place a child in your home?

Midtwenties me was single and ready to mingle in Newport Beach, California. I was supposed to go on a first date with Matt, whom I casually nicknamed "Hot Surfer Dude." I had a small cold (that I may have dramatized to him earlier in the day), and he ended up canceling because he has a thing with germs. I guess being in range of a woman with the sniffles was not the ideal first date.

Feeling bummed, I called my parents. As I rambled, my other line beeped, and I decided to answer the call. It was Matt calling to apologize and invite me out to dinner that night. I accepted. Responding to Matt's phone call changed things for me. It triggered a relationship that has included a marriage (thirteen years and going strong), the gift of parenthood with two beach-loving kids, and cofounding multiple businesses that have reached millions of people.

That call marked an important moment on the timeline of our relationship. If I hadn't answered, I might have been stuck in my disappointment or delayed my dream come true.

Similarly (without the germ drama), God is calling you. First, He's inviting you into a relationship with Him. And second, He's asking if you're ready to make an impact for Him. He wants to transform your heart, mind, and will to align with His so you will keep in step with the miraculous things He wants to do.

He's inspiring you to tackle that book idea. He's inviting you to be His voice of reconciliation in a season of division and hate. He's empowering you to teach others, create, motivate, challenge societal norms, form that nonprofit, adopt, start that business, pursue that passion project, birth something new, or [fill in the blank]. God doesn't want you to be silent but to steward the resources and life He's given you. It's not time to shrink back; it's time to show up…boxing gloves and all!

## God's Divine Strategic Plan—the Best Life Plan to Follow

A strategic plan is a business document that defines an organization's vision, mission, direction, and goals, as well as the resources or action needed to pursue those objectives. This plan is often used to make decisions, empower focus, and align resources for the organization's best next steps. *Check out pages 47-49 to develop a divine strategic plan for your life. Mark that page and look at it often as you work through this book.*

In act 1 of this book, we'll look at God's divine strategic plan. We'll explore six ways God frequently lets people know what He's inviting them to do. After reading, you'll be equipped with a healthy faith foundation to hear and answer your call in this season. God is developing His dreams for you, and He's leading you by giving you direction and drawing you closer to Him.

Perhaps you picked up this book feeling directionless. That's okay. I pray God will speak through these words and provide insight. Maybe you already have a goal or dream in mind, and you're ready to take action on that thing! Cue that *Rocky* theme song—let's lay a healthy foundation of faith as you do! This firm foundation brings freedom to show up in the story God is writing. Journeying through life with Him is a radical adventure. I'm excited to be doing this with you!

## Talk to God About This

What's your game plan for reading through this book?
Schedule that time in your calendar now.

### Simple Prayer

Lord, may Your divine strategic plan in this season
become abundantly evident. Amen.

## The Next Best Adventure Step

○  To continue pursuing your purpose, keep reading to the next page.

○  Do you feel just a tiny bit selfish focusing on your dream? Read chapter 35, and then come back here to pick up where you left off.

*Don't forget to check off day 1 as complete on the contents page.*

# GOD EMPOWERS PURPOSE

*Men dream that heroes are only to be made on special occasions,
once or twice in a century; but in truth the finest heroes are home-
spun, and are more often hidden in obscurity than platformed by
public observation. Trust in the living God is the bullion out of which
heroism is coined. Perseverance in well-doing is one of the fields
in which faith grows not flowers, but the wheat of her harvest.*

CHARLES H. SPURGEON

Do you ever wonder, "What's my purpose?" If so, you're in good company—people have been asking that question throughout history. Businesses, products, and people thrive with a clear and concise purpose. In this chapter, we'll walk through a few activities to help power-punch purpose into your soul.

## Power Punch

Draw a chair below. List the different ways this chair can function. Get creative.

There are different types of chairs, and they serve various functions. You can stand on a folding chair, reaching your fancy Christmas bowl on the top shelf. You can line up your kitchen chairs to make a train for your kids. You can hold on to your recliner for balance while you do some squats. Let's be honest though—why squats when you can spend your time twirling in that office chair? I'm sure you added more to your list as well. A chair can serve many different roles and functions, but what is its primary purpose? To be a seat.

## Your Primary Purpose Provides Security and Strength to Your Various Roles

As a child of God, what is your main purpose? The Westminster Shorter Catechism, written in the 1640s, sums it up beautifully: "Man's chief end is to glorify God, and to enjoy him forever." Your purpose isn't to strive to get but to thrive as you give God glory.

Genesis 1:26-27 shows that we're created in the image of God. Throughout the Old and New Testaments, we are reminded that we're created not only *for* God's glory but also *to bring* Him glory. As we do, we see God's goodness.

> You guide me with your counsel, and afterward you will receive me to glory. Whom have I in heaven but you? And there is nothing on earth that I desire besides you. My flesh and my heart may fail, but God is the strength of my heart and my portion forever (Psalm 73:24-26).

You glorify and enjoy God in your various roles, labels, or functions. Mother, father, son, daughter, teacher, professor, pastor, grandparent, friend, spouse, single, leader, creative, author, entrepreneur...each of the labels you wear provides opportunities to fulfill your purpose. As a child of God, you aren't defined *exclusively* by those labels but by the security of knowing Christ. You live out your purpose as you rest in the day-to-day rhythms of worshipping God. The decisions you make, the action you take, and the virtues you display are all acts of worship as you seek and find Him. The pressure is off. Understanding your purpose paves the way for one of the most wonderful responses we can have—obedience.

# Power Punch

Finish drawing stick-figure you. Underneath your main purpose, add more lines and write out some of your secondary labels.

*My main purpose is* _____ .

(Hint: I highlighted it in orange on the previous page.)

## Keep the Main Thing the Main Thing

Understanding your purpose to glorify and enjoy God is paramount in the divine strategic plan. Dreams work best when they are continually saturated with purpose. As God invites you to take a step, you can confidently pursue radical, God-given dreams and callings, like moving overseas for missionary work or moving down the block to live closer to your aging parent.

When dreams are established on one of your secondary functions (like missionary or daughter) and not on your primary purpose, you may struggle with your mindset or identity as you pursue that thing. But as long as you fulfill your primary purpose—glorifying and enjoying God—in both the sacred moments and the repetitive, boring moments throughout your day, you will be headed in the right direction. As you dare to dream with God from this place, you move from a self-focused worldview to a Christ-focused one.

You may see the words "dreams," "goals," and "callings" used interchangeably throughout this book. Just know that your purpose should be central. You wear multiple hats and carry out different functions in your life, yet one primary purpose remains. No matter the season, God empowers you to live on purpose! As we sit together in that purpose, this book will help you take the next right step toward tackling one of your God-given dreams. Let's do that thing!

## Talk to God About This

Have you ever built a dream on one of your secondary functions
or titles? What was the dream? Did it become a reality?

## Simple Prayer

Lord, may my purpose—to glorify and enjoy You—
provide me with an abundance of peace. Amen.

## The Next Best Adventure Step

○  Looking to find or add fuel to your passion? Continue reading to the
next page.

○  Want to analyze your talents and gifts? Read chapter 23, and then
come back here to pick up where you left off.

*Don't forget to check off day 2 as complete on the contents page.*

# 3

# GOD ESTABLISHES PASSION IN ORDINARY, EVERYDAY LIFE

*Whatever you do, find the God-centered, Christ-exalting, Bible-saturated passion of your life, and find your way to say it and live for it and die for it. And you will make a difference that lasts. You will not waste your life.*

JOHN PIPER

Which came first in each of these pairs?

☐ the chicken
☐ the egg

☐ laughter
☐ a joke

☐ your passion
☐ the calling

Your passions reveal your calling. The very thing that makes you come alive also provokes you to action. Passion is more often caught than taught, almost as if it's infused in your DNA. My own passion for impacting others through media started in third grade. Over time I became my school's version of film-obsessed Dawson Leery from *Dawson's Creek*.

Pinpointing your passions is a great second step in understanding God's divine strategic plan for your life. Your passion may have to do with...

faith        creativity        community        business

education        animals        hobbies        social justice

empowerment        health & wellness        nature        relationships

church        traveling        [fill in the blank]

"Passion"—a strong sentiment toward something.

"Holy pain-point passion"—a phrase I made up to communicate a God-given conviction or a resilient response toward something that needs restoration.

Some passions are merely for pleasure or play, and some act as holy pain points that keep you awake at night. Every divine strategic plan is propelled by passion. God often establishes our passions as they intermingle with the fabric of ordinary, everyday life.

Throughout this book, we'll be looking at the biblical account of Moses's journey. His passion was evident at an early age, and God later highlighted it for him as significant. Moses was a God-fearing man and one of the first of many figures in the Bible who received a call from God. We can look to his account to help establish the pattern for the rest.

# Power Punch

1.  Noah was called to build _____.
2.  Mary was called to deliver _____.
3.  Jesus was called to deliver us from _____.

God called Moses to lead the Hebrew people from Egypt to Canaan and into the Promised Land. Let me set up his story. At the time of Moses's birth, Hebrews were slaves in Egypt (Genesis 15:13). Pharaoh demanded that every Hebrew newborn male should be killed (Exodus 1:15-22). A Hebrew woman gave birth to a son (later named Moses) and kept him safe by hiding him for three months. In an amazing divine turn of events, her baby was adopted by Pharaoh's daughter, and Moses was raised and educated in Pharaoh's palace and the Egyptian court. But even though he

1. an ark 2. Jesus 3. sin

grew up in in the center of Egyptian culture, his Hebrew heritage had already been established. Here's where the holy passion comes into play.

> One day, after Moses had grown up, he went out to where his own people were and watched them at their hard labor. He saw an Egyptian beating a Hebrew, one of his own people. Looking this way and that and seeing no one, he killed the Egyptian and hid him in the sand (Exodus 2:11-12 NIV).

Moses had such deep compassion for the Hebrew man that he killed the Egyptian. He defended the oppressed. How would you define Moses's holy pain-point passion—equality? Justice? Freedom?

Now, I'm not suggesting we murder someone because of our passion. Pause and take a closer look at what we just read. Moses's passion was so ingrained in him that he fought, suffered, and sacrificed *everything*.

When Moses was outed as a murderer, he feared Pharaoh's punishment and fled to the desert of Midian, where he later got married, had two sons, and took care of his father-in-law's sheep. In chapter 4, we'll pick up the story forty years later when Moses is eighty. We'll see how God uses this passion to push Moses toward a critical calling.

Sometimes, you don't notice your holy pain-point passion until God puts a spotlight on it or it bubbles to the surface with a desire for divine justice. Other times, your passion causes a wrestling match between your mind and your will, and you wonder what the junk you're supposed to do next. As you consider the ordinary moments in your day, you may begin to sense what God has in store for you.

So if you are trying to figure out what your dream is in this season, figuring out your passions could direct you right into your God-given destiny.

## Talk to God About This

What does Moses's passion reveal about God's character?

## Simple Prayer

Lord, awaken the passions You've placed within me. Amen.

## The Next Best Adventure Step

○ Feeling reflective? To make a list of your past and present passions, read chapter 17, and then come back here to pick up where you left off.

○ Already understand your passion? Continue reading to the next page.

*Don't forget to check off day 3 as complete on the contents page.*

# 4

# GOD CREATES A PIVOT POINT

*Is your heart fixed today to recognize the presence of
God? To see His fingerprints and hear His voice? The
events that others call coincidence, will you recognize them
as sovereign providence? Ask the Lord to sharpen your
spiritual senses so that you catch a glimpse of His glory.*

PRISCILLA SHIRER

I had a firm grip on the basketball with an opportunity to win the game, but I was
trapped in the corner of the court with two defenders all up in my face. All I could
see was their jerseys, and I began to lose sight of the victory.

"Pivot!" Coach yelled.

"Pivot point"—a moment of action that propels you into a
new direction. With God, this happens in a grace-filled defining moment as you recognize Him in a new way.

As God reveals His divine strategic plan for you, you're likely to experience
pivot points. These aren't appointments you schedule or items on your to-do list—
they just find you. All you have to do is respond with your feet planted securely in
faith. Look at Moses. At eighty years old, he has a defining moment with God, and
*everything* changes.

Good ol' Moses was just shepherding around town. His primary responsibility was the safety and well-being of the flock, which may have included up to a thousand sheep. When my kids were preschoolers, I could barely herd them down the aisle at Target. I bet Mo' had his head on a swivel as he was herding those sheep to areas with good food while keeping a watchful eye out for poisonous plants and wild beasts. He's managing a lot. As he shepherds someone else's flocks, stewarding his boss's vision, he experiences a pivot point. He is called to become another type of shepherd, one who leads God's flock.

> The angel of the LORD appeared to him in a flame of fire out of the midst of a bush. He looked, and behold, the bush was burning, yet it was not consumed. And Moses said, "I will turn aside to see this great sight, why the bush is not burned." When the LORD saw that he turned aside to see, God called to him out of the bush, "Moses, Moses!" And he said, "Here I am." Then he said, "Do not come near; take your sandals off your feet, for the place on which you are standing is holy ground." And he said, "I am the God of your father, the God of Abraham, the God of Isaac, and the God of Jacob." And Moses hid his face, for he was afraid to look at God (Exodus 3:2-6).

In the course of Moses's daily sheep-wrangling activities, he has an encounter with God. It was common for bushes to catch fire in the desert—that's not what the shock and awe is in this passage. What's special is that it's the first time the Bible connects the word "holy" to God.

Sometimes our most significant pivot points look like interruptions. The bush was burning, yet it wasn't consumed. God revealed His holiness in a way it had never been revealed before. Moses catches a glimpse of heaven invading earth, and God uses this moment to draw him into sacred space.

What does Moses do? Does he divert his gaze, laser-focused on his responsibilities? Does he yawn and walk right by, unimpressed? Does he grab the nearest bucket of water, or call 911, or stop, drop, and roll? No. He recognizes this moment as holy, and he chooses to enter in.

Understand this: Nothing changed until Moses pivoted toward God. That's when God began to reveal Himself.

I pivoted to God during a holy encounter with Him in a conference prayer room in 2016. I felt His supernatural presence cover me as He reminded me to dream bigger and to trust that He's got this dream thing covered. From that moment forward, I not only saw God as trustworthy, I *experienced* Him as trustworthy too.

Have you ever sensed that an apparent interruption might be something more? Have you "turned aside" and then said "here I am" to God? By responding to these pivot points, you can take a step toward defining your calling, who you're meant to be, and the destiny you carry. These moments are gateways to repentance, invitations to redemption, and reminders of God's goodness. They are unexpected moments when Holy Spirit appears in our ordinary, everyday lives. Sometimes you barely hear the quiet whisper, and sometimes you're half-blinded by a burning bush. Either way,

**GOD'S CALLING ON YOUR LIFE IS NOT ONE-SIDED. IT REQUIRES YOUR RESPONSE AND ACTION.**

these life-changing moments happen when you "turn aside" and say "Here I am." God calls, you respond.

So what happened in that basketball game? When my coach yelled to pivot, I responded by planting one foot on the ground and taking one step with the other. As I squeezed between the defenders, I saw an opening and passed the ball to a teammate who took the winning shot just as the clock ran out. Talk about a middle-school triumph! Obviously, we celebrated by dancing and singing around the court, just like that scene from *High School Musical*. Okay, maybe we didn't, but you hear what I'm saying, right? Everything changed with that pivot.

When God calls your name, pay attention.

## *Talk to God About This*

Have you ever had a "Here I am" pivot point
with God? What was it like?

## Simple Prayer

Lord, give me the strength to pivot
toward You as You call. Amen.

## The Next Best Adventure Step

- ○ To consider what pulls on your heartstrings, continue reading to the next page.

- ○ Looking for your pivot-point moment? Read chapter 18, and then come back here to pick up where you left off.

*Don't forget to check off day 4 as complete on the contents page.*

# 5

# GOD CALLS OUT THE PROBLEM

*Our greatest fear should not be of failure but of*
*succeeding at things in life that don't really matter.*

FRANCIS CHAN

People who work in marketing often use the classic "let's pull on their heartstrings" technique. Great marketers and brands make it a goal to make a relational connection—specifically, by pinpointing a problem the potential customer may be experiencing. For example, an advertisement may start off by establishing one problem. If the potential customer connects to the problem, they'll most likely want to hear how a product or idea can bring a solution.

## Power Punch

Pretend you're the potential customer and circle the problems below:

- "Disappointed because your child is struggling to go to bed every night? This app is guaranteed to retrain your child's habits and have them asleep sooner so you can actually enjoy some 'me time.'"

- "How can you keep your dream alive if it's draining your bank account? This course will show you how to monetize your passion with purpose so you can keep doing what you love while making an impact."

- "Are you overwhelmed with a messy house? This easy-to-use system will transform your home from chaos to clutter-free in just seven minutes a day."

The customer can relate to the simple messaging. It connects to their heart and provides hope that a solution is possible. Calling out a problem creates a need for a solution—I'm pretty sure this is a God strategy too.

## After Moses Said "Here I Am," This Happened

> Then the LORD said, "I have surely seen the affliction of my people who are in Egypt and have heard their cry because of their taskmasters. I know their sufferings" (Exodus 3:7).

Right after Moses responded to God's voice and said, "Here I am!" he remained still and listened. Then God began to affirm the very thing that Moses was so passionate about. God connected to Moses's heart even before He communicated Moses's calling.

As God was confirming the passion and problems that hurt Moses's heart, imagine how known and seen Moses must have felt. God was saying, "Yes, Moses, I know their pain. I see it too." God was telling Moses He cared. He was affirming Moses's passion as holy. He established a connection with Moses by confirming the problem. Highlighting the problem was first, and the calling came second for Moses.

## Language Is Developed in the Listening

Clearly, God does a lot of stuff behind the scenes before He plants dreams in our hearts. He prepares us before sending us to go and do. He establishes connection, He helps us to feel seen and heard, He affirms our passion, and He encourages our hearts. Take time to "turn aside"—to rest in these connecting moments and to reflect on them.

When God calls, pause to listen. Quiet your heart and actively listen to God's vision. That will help launch His calling for you and empower you to fulfill it. Listening to God will clarify His divine strategic plan for you. His words will inspire you when you don't feel like showing up; they will propel you when you feel more like giving up.

I've had to learn to slow down in my conversations with God. In those moments of stillness, He often speaks to my frustrations or fears and casts vision by highlighting specific problems or pain points. I don't always realize He's sharing with me things that will later connect to my calling, but as I reflect back, I can piece it together.

## When a Heart Connection Causes Action

God says, "I have surely seen the affliction...and have heard their cry...I know their suffering." Just as He did for Moses, He can highlight struggles similar to the ones that have been on your heart. This not only reveals His vision but also shows you how to align with it. Living in a world of brokenness, I've found that many things can break our hearts. But what also prompts you to act? In other words, what distresses you so much that you feel moved to do something about it? Is it the lack of leadership on your kid's sports team, which motivates you to step in and coach? Is it the mistreatment of animals, prompting you to serve at the animal shelter?

The last place my new friend Marsha wanted to volunteer was in women's ministry. As a young mom herself, she was regularly attending Bible studies at church, but she knew she needed something more. Over time, God began to show her that as she served in children's ministry, she cherished the time she spent with the moms before and after she was "on duty." They would talk about motherhood and the challenges that come with it. Marsha was developing a love for these women and helping them connect to God...and she found she actually *enjoyed* it!

Marsha caught God's vision. When she was invited to serve as the women's ministry director, her heart and soul had already connected with the women's pain points, and she was able to confidently and joyfully step into this position. God had spent years preparing Marsha's heart before He invited her to lead her local women's ministry.

How can you catch a vision of what your calling might look like? As you slow down to listen to God, He will affirm your vision and align your steps so you're ready for the things to come. Just as in infancy, language is developed in the listening. In the stillness, safety, and comfort of your relationship with your heavenly Father, you develop language. Language of promise, passion, and a desire to pursue holiness.

From this place, Holy Spirit begins to show you a glimpse into the bigger picture of purpose and how you get to glorify Him in it.

What is your story? What has God been preparing you for all along? Like Moses, you may feel as if your dream has ended. But keep your eyes and ears open to the things that pull on your heartstrings, and be ready to turn aside when God calls.

## Talk to God About This

Has God highlighted a problem that pulls on your heart? Write out that vision on page 47.

## Simple Prayer

Lord, may my heart beat in sync with Yours. Amen.

## The Next Best Adventure Step

- ○ To catch more vision, continue reading to the next page.

- ○ If you need your vision and heart checked, read chapter 20, and then come back here to pick up where you left off.

*Don't forget to check off day 5 as complete on the contents page.*

# 6

# GOD CASTS VISION INTO YOUR FUTURE

*If you don't know where you're going, you might not get there.*
YOGI BERRA

Details matter—but not when you're in the beginning stages of awakening that dream. Details. Are. Debilitating. If you handed me a bullet-point checklist of to-dos the day after I heard my calling to cofound a ministry, I would have turned it into a "to don't" so fast. The technical terms would have seemed like a foreign language to me. The only thing I needed was God's vision, not a 284-page manifesto on how to start a nonprofit. A clear vision keeps people encouraged to push through that checklist, which comes later.

We have seen that God connected to Moses's heart over the injustice the Israelites were suffering. Now He begins to cast a vision for the future. God reveals that He will rescue His chosen people from Egypt, and he explains that Moses will play a part. Just as a vision in our heart nurtures a dream, a vision for the future helps us discover God's divine strategic plan.

## Power Punch

In the Scripture below, circle God's role and underline Moses's role.

> I have come down to deliver them out of the hand of the Egyptians and to bring them up out of that land to a good and broad land, a land flowing with milk

and honey, to the place of the Canaanites, the Hittites, the Amorites, the Per-
izzites, the Hivites, and the Jebusites. And now, behold, the cry of the people
of Israel has come to me, and I have also seen the oppression with which the
Egyptians oppress them. Come, I will send you to Pharaoh that you may bring
my people, the children of Israel, out of Egypt (Exodus 3:8-10).

God isn't telling Moses to "turn left at that first giant sand dune; then go right
for 23.1 miles toward the wilderness until you hit the Red Sea. Then wave your rod
around and see what happens." Rather, God is casting a big, generic vision of what's
going to happen. "Bring my people out of Egypt." That's it.

It reminds me of the memes that show a picture of a job gone wrong with the
text, "You had one job."

Moses has one job, and God has the rest. Sometimes big vision carries big responsibility, so God begins by assuring Moses that God is the one orchestrating and leading the whole operation. God says, "Come, I will send you." Moses just gets to
respond.

**GOD IS DOING THE RESCUING, AND HE INVITES YOU TO FOLLOW HIS LEAD.**

Of course, you're not a biblical character who will travel around the wilderness
for forty years. But you can apply this part of the story to your own situation: Pursuing your call isn't really about you; it's about loving and serving God with open hands
and a willing heart, ready to influence those around you.

Yes, this is sometimes hard to do, and we'll work through some common obstacles later. But what I love about God is that He didn't fluff up Moses's ego with a pep
band and confetti poppers (although I'm pretty sure that would have been awesome). As God cast a big vision, He affirmed that He was the main character of the
story. Moses was secondary.

You've probably figured out that this isn't a self-help book. Self-help books say,
"You are enough." The gospel says, "Christ is enough." Do you see the difference?
Your strength is in Him as you discover His purpose and plan for this season.

This is how you can tackle those nitty-gritty details in your dream without getting derailed. God is casting vision over your thing. Soon He will release you to go, He'll provide the resources you need, and He'll empower you on the adventure! Prayerfully ask God for vision and write it down in His divine strategic plan on page 47. Utilize this as foundational revelation as God moves you forward.

**YOUR STRENGTH TO STEP INTO YOUR DREAM IS FOUND IN GOD, NOT IN YOU.**

## Talk to God About This

What vision has God given you for the dream you're pursuing in this right-now season?

## Simple Prayer

Lord, help me catch Your vision and simple direction for the future. Amen.

## The Next Best Adventure Step

○ Ready, set, go to the next page and keep reading.

○ "Oh no! I still feel visionless; can you help?" Read chapter 33, and then come back here to pick up where you left off.

*Don't forget to check off day 6 as complete on the contents page.*

# 7

## GOD SENDS YOU

*If I could give you information of my life, it would be to show
how a woman of very ordinary ability has been led by God in
strange and unaccustomed paths to do in His service what
He has done in her. And if I could tell you all, you would see
how God has done all, and I nothing. I have worked hard, very
hard, that is all; and I have never refused God anything.*

FLORENCE NIGHTINGALE

Asian street food of dumplings, fried rice, pork belly wrapped in fluffy clouds of
delight, and veggies overflowed our plates. As our family of four sat at one of our
favorite restaurants, Max, my then seven-year-old, announced that this was his least-
favorite place ever. I think the green stuff on his plate had something to do with
it...and the fact that the menu didn't include the classic staple to his diet—the pea-
nut butter and jelly sandwich.

The restaurant is run by a family that we consider royalty in our town. Not only
are they the kindest people who make delicious food, but on this particular day, one
member of their family gave one member of our family some much-needed momentum. The Grandma of the Restaurant came to greet us, asking how we were enjoying
the meal. We told her how much we love their food...and then she noticed my son's
plate. His fork hadn't been moved. The rice was untouched, the greens neglected.

She simply stood by my son, smiling at him. She "grandma-ed" this moment so
hard. The stand-still-smile went on for minutes. In the uncomfortable silence, my

husband and I gave each other *that* look. You know, the one that says you don't know whether a situation is amazing or absurd.

And then we experienced a history-making moment.

My son picked up his fork and began shoving green food into his face. Fueled with a fear I can only describe as holy, Max ate nutritious food as if this was his last meal on earth. The Grandma of the Restaurant smiled and walked off like the queen that she is. I almost did the holy hustle, declaring this moment a miracle from God.

Just being in some people's presence can motivate action. For my son, it was the Grandma of the Restaurant. For runners, it could be a pacer. It could be a teacher, coach, mentor, or boss. But

## BEING IN THE PRESENCE OF GOD INVITES US TO ACTION.

most of all, being in God's presence invites us to action. God is more than a coach or boss. He's an all-powerful, all-knowing, fully-present God who is inviting you into His story. He's saying to us what He said to Moses: "Come."

> Come, I will send you to Pharaoh that you may bring my people, the children of Israel, out of Egypt (Exodus 3:10).

The word "come" implies that we are cooperating with what God is already doing. It is a way of saying, "Join me!" No one says "come" if they are staying behind. So when God tells Moses to come, He is inviting Moses to partner with Him in something bigger than himself. When God sends us, He doesn't send us *apart* from Himself—He sends us *with* Himself. He goes before us and stands beside us. Therefore, "come" is an empowering word. It reminds us that God invites us to join in what He is planning to do!

Moses is not being commissioned and sent out based on his experience in the palace, his initiative, or his leadership potential. He's being invited to trust that God will equip him in this calling. You might not always be able to see or feel the forward momentum, but it's always present in the kingdom of God and will be until we're face to face with Jesus.

"Come"—an invitation to join God in what He has decided to do. God already knows the outcome, and He's leading you toward it.

As you've started to work through the divine strategic plan, you've been meeting with God and catching His vision. He is empowering you to glorify and enjoy Him as you prepare to see His dream for you come true. My hope and prayer are that you will hear Him say, "Come with Me."

Of course, this happens in salvation, but other "come with me" moments happen repeatedly as God invites us into new adventures. I experienced one when a pastor prayed for my family, and through His words I felt the presence of God confirm a move. You may experience that moment while crying your eyes out during worship, while reading a Scripture passage that stands out to you, or while God speaks confirming words through your local church leaders or friends.

God is commissioning you and sending you in a new direction. He sends out ordinary men and women, young and old, to follow Him as He brings them to territory that is new to them but familiar to Him. God is the GPS guiding the journey—will you hear His prompts? How will you respond? Moses compiled a long list of excuses, which we will tackle in act 2.

## Power Punch

Maybe you've already heard God say "Come with Me." Ask God to highlight for you how you're responding, and check off the items that apply to you.

☐ You got so excited, you're all in, running miles ahead...and bulldozing a new lane God hadn't set for you.

☐ You're comparing yourself to people around you, wondering why their plates are overflowing as you hunger for more—more opportunity, more resources, more finances, more [fill in the blank]. Comparisons will leave you craving things that God in His wisdom hasn't given you.

☐ You're in excuse mode, wondering why in the world He called you anyway.

☐ You know God sent you and is equipping you into something important. You're learning to trust Him fully.

Running at your own pace will get you out of step, but running at God's pace keeps you in stride with His will. Remember, God is doing the rescuing and leading; He's setting the pace. God is sending you. Spend time in His presence today; He's lovingly inviting you to take action in some areas...green veggies optional.

## Talk to God About This

What dream or goal is God inviting you to move toward?

## Simple Prayer

Lord, help me to trust
Your leadership and plan. Amen.

## The Next Best Adventure Step

○ "Is now the right season for my dream?" Read chapter 19, and then come back here to pick up where you left off.

○ "I'm ready to respond to God!" Turn the page and keep reading.

*Don't forget to check off day 7 as complete on the contents page.*

# 8

# WILL YOU LET GOD LEAD AND ANSWER THE CALL?

*God is not looking for the perfect words. He
is looking for perfect submission.*

JOSHUA DUBOIS

*Congrats on making it through Act 1 and setting a healthy foundation for your
God-given dream! Go send a text or message to your accountability partner letting
them know how far you made it.*

☐ Okay, I'm totally a pro dreamer.          ☐ Nah, I'm pro...crastinating.

At the end of this chapter, you'll find a place to record the divine strategic plan for the dream you're tackling in this season. You may have already worked through some of it. Dog-ear those pages and revisit them often as you work through this book. The goal is to have this plan complete by the end of the book. This can be something you reference when you need a spiritual kick in the pants to keep showing up. You can also find a downloadable version at www.jennyrandle.com/dream.

We need to be the artists, worshippers, teachers, and communicators who are influencing culture and shifting people's eyes to Christ. We need to be the leaders and industry shapers who are changing the nation and world because we understand this concept of hearing God's voice, we know how to dream, and we are walking in our calling. We often limit ourselves based on our own abilities and on the things we see right in front of us. What if we were able to work through the hard stuff, see God as bigger than the obstacles, and know that because of Him we're able to risk?

So here's the big question. Will you let God lead, and will you answer the call? My hope is that by now God has spoken some encouragement to your soul and that you have a goal to pursue in your own life or to help another person achieve. What is that dream?

My dad had a dream to complete an Ironman triathlon—swimming 2.4 miles, biking 112 miles, and running 26.2 miles. He trained for hours upon hours every day for months. He sacrificed his time, energy, and finances, and he worked on his mental stamina to complete such a feat.

When he started training, he couldn't even swim 25 yards at the pool. He had to learn how to swim properly, and he had to overcome the fear and anxiety of swimming for miles among 2,600 people! Every night, Dad would stick his face in a sink of water and hold his breath while listening to a recording of himself saying, "You are a powerful swimmer." (He also had to sacrifice his pride as we laughed about his wet and wild pep-talk to himself!)

Have you ever watched people compete in an Ironman? I just about collapsed from exhaustion just typing that. Racers are given seventeen hours to finish, and my dad finished with hours to spare. After we celebrated his victory, we hung out at the finish line as the clock was ticking toward the seventeen-hour mark.

I'll never forget watching one competitor—a woman in her midseventies. She was in way better shape than I've ever been in. Yards from the finish, her body gave out, and she fell to the pavement. But she was determined. This powerhouse of a woman began dragging herself toward the finish line. As she crawled across the finish line, beating that seventeen-hour mark, the crowd exploded in applause, and I was a blubbering mess. Something magical happens when you walk in righteousness and do whatever it takes to achieve your dream.

One of the best ways you can bring God glory is to be obedient in the things He calls you to. How will you need to train to make sure you cross the finish line? Yes, there will be roadblocks, and you may sometimes feel as if you're drowning or dragging yourself across the pavement. God never said that achieving your dream would be easy. Be intentional to keep showing up. One foot in front of the other, friend. God's got this!

## Talk to God About This

How is success measured in your God-given dream?

## Simple Prayer

Lord, thank You for inviting me to pursue this dream...and
for giving me courage to say yes. Amen.

## The Next Best Adventure Step

○ If you flat-out said no to pursuing that dream, read chapter 32, and
then come back here to pick up where you left off.

○ To rest in assurance from God, turn to the next chapter and keep
reading.

*Don't forget to check off day 8 as complete on the contents page.*

# Divine Strategic Plan

**My Dream** (chapter 18)                          Start Date

**My Purpose** (chapter 2)                    **Whom I Serve** (chapter 20)

**The Problem that Moves Me to Action** (chapter 5)

**My Future Vision** (chapter 6)

## My Driving Passions (chapters 3, 17)

## My Tangible Goals (chapter 22)

# Internal Factors (Act 2)

My Excuses

God's Assurances

# Start Doing (chapters 25, 26, 27)

| Three Major Tasks | Resources I'll Need | Due Date |
| --- | --- | --- |
| | | |

# DITCH THE DOUBT AND DREAM WITH GOD.

# Act 2

Nightmare Excuses
or Peaceful Assurance

# 9

# INTRODUCTION TO ACT 2

*This is why the Word of God is so essential in the daily, ongoing life of a believer. Because from the minute you close your Bible in the morning, you're entering a world that's fighting every truth and teaching it represents. At every turn. And if God's message is not deep inside you, where you can meditate on it, return to it, and frequently call it back to mind, you won't be able to discern what's really true from what may be really intriguing, really alluring, really convincing, but really false. And really defeating.*

MATT CHANDLER

In any great narrative, there are plot twists, roadblocks, and nightmares. This is the part of the story where we discuss the brokenness of humanity. Dreamer, welcome to act 2. The place our sleepy dreams cause us to toss and turn in the darkness of night.

"Hey, Mom, there's a pile of free crap over there." My third-grade son points out the car window to a mini junkyard in front of someone's house.

Typically, we don't go around town yelling about crap, but as I turned my head to where he was pointing, I couldn't contain my laughter. The residents had created a dumpster dive in their front yard and topped it off with a cardboard sign that read "crap free."

How many of us so effortlessly call out our garbage like that? In act 1, we talked about how God leads us in our calling. There was Moses, having a holy-moment encounter with God. A life-defining moment. And then what does he do? Does he say yes to God and run off in a ninja suit to save the Israelites from their suffering?

No! He pivots toward God and listens but is slow to actually take a step. He begins to make a ton of excuses, one after another. He doesn't water down his feelings or compartmentalize them to deal with later. He spills his guts with authenticity and goes to God in his doubt and discomfort. Moses enters into some hard conversations with God.

As I studied Moses's excuses in Exodus 3 and 4, I saw many similarities between his excuses and the ones I've made when considering my God-given dreams. There's a crap pile of reasons why people don't pursue their dream come true. If we don't look at the brokenness for what it is (often paralyzing and self-consuming), we'll just pretend to be something we're not.

## Let's Over-Spiritualize This Moment

Let's not look the other way but point right at our excuses and call them what they are. *Sin. Shame. Insecurity. Doubt.* It's time for us to be dreamers who are willing to get uncomfortable as we let God lead in our calling.

So back to the garbage pile and sign my son found. It was a picture-worthy moment, so I grabbed my phone and snapped a photo to share with my internet besties. Upon further investigation, falling off the corner of the sign was the very edge of an "S." The sign actually said, "scrap free." Yes, I'm going to so over-spiritualize this moment for us.

> [God will] provide for those who grieve in Zion—to bestow on them a crown of beauty instead of ashes, the oil of joy instead of mourning, and a garment of praise instead of a spirit of despair. They will be called oaks of righteousness, a planting of the LORD for the display of his splendor (Isaiah 61:3 NIV).

Look at the signs in your life. The things you may have labeled as garbage, your excuses, the things you discarded or forgot about...they're all pieces of something bigger. They're pointing to an opportunity for restoration.

Moses acknowledged his weakness, so let's take some time together to do the same. Let's look honestly at our brokenness but also remember that because we know Christ, we can rest in His assurance of forgiveness and restoration. Let's enter into hard conversations with God over the next few days and find out where we have been holding on to our excuses and where we have been clinging to Christ.

## Talk to God About This

What has been in your pile of excuses for not
working on a God-given dream?

## Simple Prayer

Lord, help me face my excuses and brokenness,
receive Your grace, and be restored. Amen.

## The Next Best Adventure Step

○ "I need friend support, and stat!" Read chapter 21, and then come back here to pick up where you left off.

○ Ready to tackle excuse number one? If so, turn the page and keep reading.

*Don't forget to check off day 9 as complete on the contents page.*

# 10

# I'M A NOBODY

*If you look at the world, you'll be distressed. If you look within,*
*you'll be depressed. If you look at God, you'll be at rest.*

CORRIE TEN BOOM

One of my favorite photos is of my Italian grandmother, Nonna, and my cousin. They are both smiling but also fiercely determined, elbows resting on the table and arms upright. They're about to have an arm-wrestling contest—one of the great battles in our family's history (okay, that may be a slight exaggeration).

When you zoom in to a digital photo, you see a mosaic of individual squares of color. As you zoom out, you stop focusing on each small pixel and start to see the big picture. Our world is made up of pixels, from the little everyday occurrences to the huge life events that can build or break us. We often view our world by focusing on one of these pixels at a time, missing the tapestry of God's big story unfolding all around us.

As Moses stood on holy ground, he had one-pixel vision. God was revealing His big-picture calling on Moses's life, but Moses focused on his own limitations. Here's his first excuse:

> But Moses said to God, "Who am I that I should go to Pharaoh and bring the children of Israel out of Egypt?" (Exodus 3:11).

It's not clear if Moses was throwing a pity party, or if he felt like a nobody, or if he was genuinely self-aware and wondering, *Who am I?* I mean, imagine what it would take to lead more than a million people from where they have lived for 430 years. I can barely take our kids on a walk around the neighborhood without a map or minor meltdown.

I love this passage because again, God didn't puff up Moses's ego or launch sparklers of fun to celebrate. As Moses is wondering about his ability to accomplish what the Lord set before him, God makes this reply:

> But I will be with you, and this shall be the sign for you, that I have sent you: when you have brought the people out of Egypt, you shall serve God on this mountain (Exodus 3:12).

We often make disqualifying statements and excuses that prevent us from living on purpose. "Woe is me!" "Who am I?" We act as if we live for the accolades and praise of people. Our society looks at the "somebodies" who have fame and fortune as examples of strength and success. Our God looks at the "nobodies" who are unqualified but dependent. It's not in our strength the dream comes true, but God's.

The problem arises when we focus on one pixel—"Who am I?" The doubters focus on the disqualifying statement, but the doers look at the One who qualifies. As the Scripture shares, Moses felt small with a big call. God simply reminds Moses that God is even bigger than the calling and that He will be with him. God points Moses to Himself

**OUR MINDSET SHOULDN'T BE, "WHO AM I TO DO THIS THING?" BUT RATHER, "GOD, WHO ARE YOU?" GOD WILL REMIND YOU OVER AND OVER AGAIN THAT HE IS WITH YOU.**

while continuing to cast a vision for Moses's calling. Like Moses, we all need the reminder that God is bigger than anything He is calling us to.

What if this is on purpose? What if God calls us to something bigger so that we lean into His strength to accomplish our calling? God can do way more with a nobody than any person can do with a somebody.

| My Excuse | God's Assurance |
|:---:|:---:|
| I say,<br>"I'm a nobody." | God responds,<br>"I will be with you." |

When my dad was a young boy, his father was in the United States Army. This meant my dad's parents had to talk with their kids about some things most families don't have to discuss. My grandpa was born and raised in the United States. Nonna was from Italy, where her prosperous family owned several stores and orchards. Being raised in different countries, and having been stationed all around the world, they faced a difficult decision. What would happen to their young family if my grandpa died? They agreed that Nonna would raise their kids in the United States if anything were to happen.

Twelve years into her marriage, she was widowed, unemployed, and caring for four children (ages eleven, six, three, and three months) in Germany. The easy answer for Nonna would have been to return to her hometown in Italy and the comforts she once knew. She would have received help with the children and support from her family and friends. But Nonna had promised her husband that she would raise their children in the United States, and she remained committed to fulfilling this dream of a better life for them.

Can you imagine losing a spouse and moving your grieving young family to another continent, hoping for a better life? From the outside looking in, this doesn't seem like any dream you'd add to your bucket list. Yet this defining moment changed everything for their family.

I don't know if she felt like a nobody as she moved to a foreign country. Or if she felt small compared to the big commitment she had made to her husband. I'm not sure what excuses she fought. But I do know that she understood that God was with her. Nonna's faith was foundational. She was at church every opportunity she got, and God provided her the strength and comfort that stabilized her family.

Zoom out from that one-pixel vision, dreamer. You are a part of God's story. Even when you wonder who you are, or you second-guess your calling, rest in the assurance that He is with you. God is providing you stability and strength, just like he did for Moses, and just like He did for my Nonna.

And yes, you better believe she won that arm-wrestling contest.

## Talk to God About This

Do you have one-pixel vision? Are you focusing
on yourself and your own abilities?

## Simple Prayer

Lord, give me eyes to see You. Amen.

## The Next Best Adventure Step

○ To face another excuse and find assurance to overcome it, turn the page and keep reading.

○ Wondering if your dream requires you to hustle or overwork? Read chapter 34, and then come back here to pick up where you left off.

*Don't forget to check off day 10 as complete on the contents page.*

# 11

# I DON'T KNOW ENOUGH

*The gospel is this: We are more sinful and flawed in ourselves than we ever dared believe, yet at the very same time we are more loved and accepted in Jesus Christ than we ever dared hope.*

TIMOTHY KELLER

The other day one of my kids, who will remain nameless, kept getting out of bed. You know what followed them out of that bed? A whole pile of questions and time-wasting tactics.

"Can I get a drink of water?"

"What makes the sky blue?"

And the mother of all excuses: "I don't know how to sleep. Why do I have to?"

How often do we pull similar shenanigans and stall tactics as we're sleepwalking through our dream? "What if people realize I don't have those credentials?" "What if I fail my real estate test?" "Am I even smart enough to do this?" "What if I don't have the right theological answer for that person?" "What if I just don't know enough?"

Well, I guess those of us who ask questions like these are in good company. We've seen that Moses phrased his first excuse to God as a question: "Who am I?" Staying on trend, he now asks, "Who are You?"

> Then Moses said to God, "If I come to the people of Israel and say to them, 'The God of your fathers has sent me to you,' and they ask me, 'What is his name?' what shall I say to them?" God said to Moses, "I AM WHO I AM." And he

said, "Say this to the people of Israel: 'I AM has sent me to you.'" God also said to Moses, "Say this to the people of Israel: 'The LORD, the God of your fathers, the God of Abraham, the God of Isaac, and the God of Jacob, has sent me to you.' This is my name forever, and thus I am to be remembered throughout all generations" (Exodus 3:13-15).

I find it hilariously uncomfortable how God basically responds to Moses (and us) the same way I responded to my kids' questions. "Because I said so." It's the classic Parenting 101 response that I'm sure all parents have used. My husband and I have authority over our kids' nighttime shenanigans. "I said so" translates to "My answer is sufficient to your questions. Do you trust me? I love you so much and know what's best for you, so do as I say. I'm in charge."

**WE REST IN THE ASSURANCE OF WHO HE IS. WHO HE'S CREATED US TO BE IS SECONDARY.**

Or as God says, "I AM WHO I AM."

God holds the highest authority, so it totally makes sense for Him to pull the "because I said so" card. He's in charge. When we make an excuse, like "I don't know enough," God responds by merely telling us that He does. He knows the future, the past, and the present. He's outside of time, yet He created time. God is alive, immediate, and present. He knows what's best, so we need to do what He says.

*My Excuse*
I say,
"I don't know enough."

*God's Assurance*
God responds,
"I am who I am."

"I AM WHO I AM," or "I WILL BE WHAT I WILL BE." The phrase "I am he" occurs multiple times in the Old Testament (for example, see Isaiah 41:4; 43:10; 48:12). In Isaiah 46:4 (NIV) God says to the people of Israel, "Even to your old age and gray hairs I am he, I am he who will sustain you. I have made you and I will carry you; I will sustain you and I will rescue you."

In the New Testament, Jesus boldly brings this full circle: "Truly, truly, I say to you, before Abraham was, I am" (John 8:58). Jesus stood before the Jews and claimed to be the same "I am" who spoke to Moses as he stood on holy ground. And He's the same "I am" who stands with us today, saying, "Unless you believe that I am he you will die in your sins" (John 8:24).

# Power Punch

The Gospel of John includes seven "I am" statements:

- I am the bread of life (John 6:35,41,48,51).
- I am the light of the world (John 8:12).
- I am the door (John 10:7,9).
- I am the good shepherd (John 10:11,14).
- I am the resurrection and the life (John 11:25).
- I am the way, and the truth, and the life (John 14:6).
- I am the true vine (John 15:1,5).

May these "I am" statements always remind us who has authority over our lives. You can fully trust Jesus as He brings you life, frees you from sin, guides you out of darkness, sustains, watches and protects you, leads you into all truth, and equips you to bear fruit.

So when you say, "I don't know enough," you're right. You don't. You don't know what will happen tomorrow, let alone five months from now. You don't know when your last breath will be, and you don't know how to heal all of humanity. So what?

It's not about you; it's about the God who sent you. The revelation you have in "I AM" is enough.

## Talk to God About This

When did you last thank Jesus for who He is? Identify the qualities that make Him trustworthy.

## Simple Prayer

Lord, forgive me for letting my lack of knowledge hold me back from trusting You. Amen.

## The Next Best Adventure Step

○ Ever wonder if people doubt your dream or calling? Turn the page and keep reading.

○ Do you think "I'm powerful and enough" is a complete thought? Read chapter 36, and then come back here to pick up where you left off.

*Don't forget to check off day 11 as complete on the contents page.*

# 12

# I DON'T THINK THEY'LL BELIEVE ME

*If you live for people's acceptance, you'll die from their rejection.*
LECRAE MOORE

As God continues to give the one-two punch to Moses's excuses, Exodus 3 concludes with a detailed play-by-play of how He would free the Israelites. God told Moses what to say to the Israelites and added that they would respond favorably. Then He explained that the only way the king of Egypt would let the Israelites go was if God intervened, and He reassured Moses that He would provide deliverance with His mighty hand. The king will eventually agree to let the Israelites leave, and God's favor will tangibly be on them. The Egyptians will then provide silver, gold, and many additional resources, and they'll be stripped of their wealth because of it.

Imagine having a talk with God like this. You're getting a divine download of wisdom and action steps. It's almost as if God is in the front of the room, mapping this out on a fancy whiteboard. How do you think Moses responded?

> Then Moses answered, "But behold, they will not believe me or listen to my voice, for they will say, 'The LORD did not appear to you'" (Exodus 4:1).

## When God Told Me to Google

In 2016, I responded to God's call to step into a speaking ministry as a profession instead of a passionate hobby. Having felt the call ten years earlier, I may have been delayed a decade because of my excuses, but I was now dedicated and determined.

As I prayed one early morning of summer, God brought out His whiteboard and began mapping out some next steps. The convo went something like this.

"Google New Jersey, creativity conference, leaders," I felt God say. Not in an audible way but in a deep, intuitive knowing sort of way. As clearly as I knew the grass was green, I know this was something I should do. The first web result was a large conference for church leaders happening three months later. Their website displayed a lineup of spiritual giants in the Christian world of authors and speakers. I felt so ill-equipped and unqualified to even think I could share space with these leaders.

In case God wasn't aware of how this typically goes down, I reminded Him. "Usually, well-known conferences like this schedule speakers a year and a half in advance. There's no way they're taking speaking proposals, let alone from a girl who hasn't written a book and who has only spoken a handful of times at leadership conferences."

God ignored my excuse and continued. "Figure out who the event coordinator is." I hacked my way through the internet and discovered his name and email. "Email him a speaking proposal on creativity in the church."

Later that day, as my kids splashed in the kiddie pool in our backyard, I wrote out the email sharing the vision God had given me and hit send.

## My Excuse

I say, "I don't think they'll believe me."

## God's Assurance

God responds, "My presence provides."

> The LORD said to him, "What is that in your hand?" He said, "A staff." And he said, "Throw it on the ground." So he threw it on the ground, and it became a serpent, and Moses ran from it. But the LORD said to Moses, "Put out your hand and catch it by the tail"—so he put out his hand and caught it, and it became a staff in his hand—"that they may believe that the LORD, the God of their fathers, the God of Abraham, the God of Isaac, and the God of Jacob, has appeared to you" (Exodus 4:2-5).

## Moses and the Magic Show

As Moses makes excuses, the Lord asks him, "What is that in your hand?" and he then begins to perform miracles. God uses signs, wonders, and miracles to lead Moses, and as a result, people see God's power on display. Our assurance isn't found in people's response toward us but in our reliance on Him.

God's presence provides provision and power. Exodus includes more than 30 miracles as God provides for Moses through his journey. Whether by instructing Moses to hit his staff on a rock for water or by releasing an army of frogs on Egypt, God provides. So how do we take this picture from Scripture and apply it to our personal situation? We can conclude that a key attribute of God is that He's a provider. Oftentimes His miracles, signs, and wonders point us to Jesus as we walk in His will. So who are we putting our faith in—people or God?

Would you like to know how the conference leader responded? The next day after sending the email, I got a lengthy reply. Here's the abridged version.

> Dear Jenny,
>
> It so happens that [insert the name of the founder of a super popular app] was supposed to be with us. Due to inevitable circumstances, he just canceled. Typically we go through our normal process of checking and reviewing our speakers intently, but I want to make an exception due to a few things: I sense your heart, and your topics match exactly what I wanted him to speak about.

The conference leader shared that this was the fastest a speaker has ever been approved and that they felt confident that God would use me to awaken creativity in church leaders. After meeting, we both sensed God's provision in this divine orchestration and celebrated this connection.

The talk I gave months later became my first book, *Courageous Creative*, and has since strengthened thousands within their divine creativity. Imagine if I hadn't reached out because of how I thought people would respond?

What is in your hand—excuses or assurance?

Do you want to share your story through a blog but worry it may offend people because you mention God? What is in your hand? What if God does a miracle and opens up conversations about His love for your readers?

Do you feel called to make organic, unprocessed, straight-from-the-farm meals for your kids, but you're hesitant because "What if they don't eat it?" But what if God performs the miracles of all miracles and they do!

Whatever what-if statement is paralyzing you, open your fist-clutched hand and place it before God. Because *what if* you trusted Him as provider?

## Talk to God About This

Are you acting on what-if excuses or trusting that God will provide?

## Simple Prayer

Lord, help me look past people's responses and find assurance by relying on You. Amen.

## The Next Best Adventure Step

○ Ever wonder if you have the skills to make this dream happen? Turn the page and keep reading.

○ Want to mark a moment you had with God? Read chapter 28, and then come back here to pick up where you left off.

*Don't forget to check off day 12 as complete on the contents page.*

# 13

## I'M NOT TALENTED ENOUGH

*God does not ask your ability. Or your inability.*
*He asks only your availability.*

MARY KAY ASH

Moses just keeps going. Here's his fourth excuse.

> But Moses said to the LORD, "Oh, my Lord, I am not eloquent, either in the past or since you have spoken to your servant, but I am slow of speech and of tongue" (Exodus 4:10).

Let's have a heart-to-heart chat about our talent and where we lack. From cleaning the bathrooms to sitting in the boardroom, when was the last time you felt like you didn't have the skills required for the job? For me, it was yesterday.

I sent my manuscript for this book to my editor a week before my second book, *Getting to Know God's Voice*, was released into the world. That book is a dream come true for me—the Holy Spirit has been a topic of interest and discovery for me for the past 20 years. It's a blessing to be able to share those words with others. However, between that book's release and this manuscript's due date, my brainpower was all used up. I'm not talented enough to juggle two big ideas and communicate them effectively at the same time.

Also, as I write this, our world is in the thick of the COVID-19 pandemic. My family hasn't gotten sick, but my kids have been sheltering all up in my space (yes, I still love them). We're also in the final stretch of the 2020 election. I'm weary; work feels heavy, holy, and meaningful; and the weight of all this wondering is just so much. I'm sure you can remember what the COVID and election season here in the United States felt like for you. It's a lot, and do any of us know how to show up for this? *Because I'm gonna need a nap now.*

As I was praying one night, I told the Lord that my mind was muddling through all the things and that I didn't have the skill set or talent to write or speak all these words I feel responsible to share. I unintentionally pulled all of Moses's excuses out of my gross-self-absorbed humanity and fell asleep wondering, *Who do I even think I am?*

If you haven't noticed, I'm writing this book in the middle of a process, not from a place of perfection. This is a judgment-free zone, okay? Please tell me I'm not alone in that thought. Have you ever felt like you don't have the skill set or are ill-equipped to pursue the plans the Lord placed before you? It's why we reject the dream, become professional procrastinators, or spend all our time preparing to do the thing instead of actually doing it.

As Moses declares himself a stuttering Stanley (as if God didn't already know), let's see how God responds.

> Then the Lord said to him, "Who has made man's mouth? Who makes him mute, or deaf, or seeing, or blind? Is it not I, the Lord? Now therefore go, and I will be with your mouth and teach you what you shall speak" (Exodus 4:11-12).

## My Excuse

I say,
"I'm not talented enough."

## God's Assurance

God responds,
"I will guide You."

As we say we're not talented enough to pursue our dream, again God reminds us of Himself. God not only fills the gaps in our brokenness but also frees us from our sin-focused and selfish tendencies. Our shortcomings or lack of skills do not disqualify us; they qualify us to have a Savior. Let me shout that again in case you're a skimmer: Your lack doesn't disqualify you from walking in your God-given calling; it qualifies you to receive what you need from Him. God is not limited by your abilities or lack of them. He is teaching, molding, and pruning you so you can display His ability. For those things to happen, you must listen and respond to His voice. I was reminded of that today.

**YOUR SHORTCOMINGS OR LACK OF SKILLS DO NOT DISQUALIFY YOU; THEY QUALIFY YOU TO HAVE A SAVIOR.**

After my night of prayer-filled, Moses-induced gut-spilling, the Lord gave me an encouraging word (on social media no less). My friend's church was live-streaming a meeting in a home. Minutes after tuning in, I heard these words from someone I've never met: "Okay, I think I have a word for Jenny Randle."

What!

"Jenny, in my mind, I saw a book cover, and you were the author. I don't know if you've ever thought about writing, but you have a wealth of information, stories, and experience, and people need to know about it."

I begin typing in the chat box as fast as my fingers would go. "I am releasing my second book in a week and writing my third one right now!"

The group leading the meeting began to cheer and thank God for this confirmation. *God sees me*, I thought. I know that fact to be true, but that day I felt it too. I was seen by a God who loves me deeply, and in that holy moment, His care for me felt palpable.

I had been rejecting my calling the night before, but as I continued watching the live stream, people continued to confirm my dream. The pastor said, "Jenny, maybe you've been feeling like you aren't qualified, and you've been thinking 'Who am I?' I feel like the Lord is saying, 'You are the one I sent.' You said yes, Jenny. God was looking for a yes. Maybe He looked to a bunch of people, but you are the one who said yes, and that qualifies you."

Tears were streaming down my cheeks. I quickly responded with affirmation that this was indeed from the Lord and that I could feel these words piercing my spirit. God used these people to confirm my calling as an author. God not only highlighted the question I was wrestling through the night before—"Who am I?"—but also strengthened me by reminding me that obedience to Him is the key.

As we read in our Scripture today, the Lord told Moses, "Now therefore go, and I will be with your mouth and teach you." May a stranger's online encouragement to me and God's message to Moses serve as reminders for you too. Your yes to God is what counts, not your natural talent (or lack of it). Do you trust He is who He says He is? When God says go and you do, He will guide you through.

God is calling those who are available. As we are learning, being available is the first step, but many people miss it because they don't have ears to hear or are distracted. As you pray this week, posture yourself to be available to God. Let Him give you a holy moment as He affirms who He has created you to be and the plan He has for your life (Ephesians 2:10). Once you become available, the next step will be actionable. We'll tackle that next step in act 3!

## Talk to God About This

Has your lack of talent helped you to depend on God?
Identify times that has happened...or could happen.

## Simple Prayer

Lord, help me respond to Your voice and be grateful
for Your faithfulness to guide me. Amen.

## The Next Best Adventure Step

○  Ready to get in position to do that thing? Read chapter 22, and then
    come back here to pick up where you left off.

○  Still making excuses? On the next page, start reading about the last
    and biggest excuse of them all.

*Don't forget to check off day 13 as complete on the contents page.*

# 14

# I DON'T WANT TO DO IT

*Complacency is a deadly foe of all spiritual growth.*

A.W. TOZER

I'm pretty sure you didn't pick up this book to get an exegetical look at the exodus of God's people. We're only touching on the beginning of the conversation between God and Moses. The Bible goes on to share that the exodus out of Egypt is not only a historical event but also a hint of what is to come—the greatest redemptive story ever told.

Some have treated this biblical passage like a self-help text. "You can find your promised land!" But we are followers of Jesus; He has found us. Moses's exchange with God reminds us that our own wilderness seasons and burning-bush moments fit into the storyline of the entire Bible.

The big picture of this narrative is that Jesus accomplished the greatest exodus of all—our deliverance from slavery to sin and the fulfillment of God's promise. Come to find out, the promised land isn't a destination to reach or a dream to achieve. It's found in the One who brings true freedom—Jesus. The story of Jesus is key to everything, including our own stories.

From our vantage point, we can see that Jesus is the answer to every one of Moses's objections.

I love the fact that during this conversation with God, Moses said the hard stuff. He didn't hide his excuses, pretending to be a man of God without fault or struggle. He was honest about his shortcomings as he stood face to face with God. Our own sin, shame, or excuses often put the conversation with God on pause because we forget the big picture. Jesus wins, and we're living in the in-between time as we wait for His return to restore all of creation.

After all, as we wait, we are called to spread the news of the gospel, knowing that God has given Jesus all authority in heaven and earth (Matthew 28:16-20). In a world that puts bad news on repeat, we could use more good news from dream chasers like you. If you have felt hemmed in or restricted by your weakness, think about this: Your relationship with God creates space and gives you unimaginable freedom. So bring each of your excuses to Him. Let Him free you to dream and to go love and serve the people He's calling you to.

As Moses pulls out the fifth and final excuse, you can feel the desperation:

> But he said, "Oh, my Lord, please send someone else" (Exodus 4:13).

If ever there was a time to use the facepalm emoji, this is the moment. If Moses did say yes to God, he would have to overcome huge obstacles, and he felt unqualified. Here's the thing: We already read that this calling wasn't based on *his* qualifications but on God's. Last I checked, God was more than qualified.

It's easier not to do that thing God invites you to, but the easy way rarely leads to lasting impact. As you discover God's story for your life, remember that He's already written the last chapter. You're just midsentence.

How does God respond to our nightmare excuses and insecurity? Here's what He said to Moses.

> Then the anger of the LORD was kindled against Moses and he said, "Is there not Aaron, your brother, the Levite? I know that he can speak well. Behold, he is coming out to meet you, and when he sees you, he will be glad in his heart. You shall speak to him and put the words in his mouth, and I will be with your mouth and with his mouth and will teach you both what to do. He shall speak

for you to the people, and he shall be your mouth, and you shall be as God to him. And take in your hand this staff, with which you shall do the signs" (Exodus 4:14-17).

God sent Aaron to help Moses, and through their journey, God provided resources, miracles, other people, wisdom, direction, and more. Finally, Moses said okay because he understood where his confidence came from. Like Moses, we can take the first step even though we still have reservations.

*My Excuse*

I say,
"I don't want to do it."

*God's Assurance*

God responds,
"I will contribute."

I had a reason for not wanting to show up for a dream. It wasn't laziness or apathy; it was fear. It's scary to show up when we face the unknown and feel out of control. I felt deep angst, but all I could say was "I just don't want to." The lie that I was going to mess it up was keeping me from hearing the voice of a loving God. A God who gently reminds us it's not really about us anyway.

When my daughter was learning to ride her bike without training wheels, she was so afraid. Every time she pedaled her bike, she let out the loudest screams you've ever heard. She felt out of control and let everyone know it. But little by little, pedal by pedal, the screams were less frequent. As her fear took a back seat, she eventually learned to ride her bike. Just last week we rode on a trail near our house and found a beautiful lake. If she had allowed her fear to stop her, she would have missed this beautiful adventure.

It is liberating to know that we are not the centerpiece of the story. Jesus is. That's why He is called the cornerstone (Acts 4:10-12). Everything finds its proper place under His lordship. So...where are you standing?

Jesus gave you full authority to put your fear and excuses in the back seat. Talk to God about the excuses you're making, and you'll find that they don't have to control you! Your excuses dissipate under the assurance and authority of Christ. As they do, you'll be empowered to enjoy the beautiful adventure God is inviting you into.

## Talk to God About This

Can you trust God to provide power and
resources for you? Why or why not?

## Simple Prayer

Lord, when things feel out of control in my calling,
remind me that You're in control. Amen.

## The Next Best Adventure Step

○ Are you focusing on your excuses or on Christ's power? To find out, continue reading on the next page.

○ Ready for action but need some on-the-job training? Read chapter 24, and then come back here to pick up where you left off.

*Don't forget to check off day 14 as complete on the contents page.*

# 15

# AM I EMBRACING MY EXCUSES
# OR CLINGING TO CHRIST?

*He that is good for making excuses is
seldom good for anything else.*

BENJAMIN FRANKLIN

Are you still sitting on the bleachers—watching others live out their God-given dreams? Every *doer* starts as a *dreamer*. Our dreams are the fuel for our actions. They motivate us to move forward. All of us have God-given dreams, but few of us have crossed the chasm from dreaming to doing. What keeps people stuck? The sticky little phrase "I can't do it." These are the devil's words, not a Christian's words!

Remember the story of Abraham and Sarah. For almost a century, this couple was plagued with infertility. Their dream was to have a child. That was a common, ordinary dream, but God had an extraordinary plan. God would in fact give them a child, but He would do more than simply fulfill their desire—He would bless the whole world through them (Genesis 12:1-3). But these things were not easy to accept. When Sarah hears about the prophetic promise, she responds in a way we all can relate to. Watch what happens!

> The LORD said, "I will surely return to you about this time next year, and Sarah your wife shall have a son." And Sarah was listening at the tent door behind him. Now Abraham and Sarah were old, advanced in years. The way of women had ceased to be with Sarah. So Sarah laughed to herself, saying, "After I am

worn out, and my lord is old, shall I have pleasure?" The LORD said to Abraham, "Why did Sarah laugh and say, 'Shall I indeed bear a child, now that I am
old?' Is anything too hard for the LORD? At the appointed time I will return to
you, about this time next year, and Sarah shall have a son." But Sarah denied it,
saying, "I did not laugh," for she was afraid. He said, "No, but you did laugh"
(Genesis 18:10-15).

Sarah hears that her long-lost dream for a child is still God's dream for her. Wonderful news, right? Well, yes...until she laughs. Have you ever heard something so
unbelievably good, you had no other reaction but to laugh? That is how Sarah felt.

But the dream wasn't so unbelievable to the Lord God. In verse 13 He asks, "Why
did Sarah laugh?" Just as Jesus marveled at His neighbors' unbelief (Mark 6:6),
the all-knowing God was astounded by Sarah's response. He didn't catch the joke
because He was obviously capable of fulfilling the dream. He might as well have
said, "What's so funny?"

Now, before you judge Sarah, remember that this narrative is not just about
Sarah. It's about us.

What if God has a dream to fulfill in you, but your reaction is to laugh it off?
Speaking in the third person, verse 14 records the Lord asking, "Is anything too hard
for the LORD?"

That's a good question. When we reject God's dream for our lives, then yes, we
are saying He is either incapable of accomplishing big things or incapable of working in our lives.

Are doubt, insecurity, or unbelief preventing you from following God as He fulfills
your calling? Take an honest assessment, and bring your deepest feelings to God.
Trust Holy Spirit to convict, correct, and comfort you.

Hundreds of years after Sarah laughed off God's dream for her, Moses struggled
to wrap his head around God's calling for him. But in the end, even though he had
no idea how long his journey would be, he finally responded to the call with obedience and let God lead.

In 2 Corinthians 3:5-6 Paul writes this to the believers in Corinth:

We don't see ourselves as capable enough to do anything in our own strength, for our true competence flows from God's empowering presence. He alone makes us adequate ministers who are focused on an entirely new covenant. Our ministry is not based on the letter of the law but through the power of the Spirit. The letter of the law kills, but the Spirit pours out life (TPT).

Well, dreamer, your nightmare excuses are ending as you begin to rest in the assurance of Christ. Your calling comes from relationship with Him. You may need to review this section (and the excuse and assurance chart on page 80) as you continue to pursue all God has for you.

So many excuses..."I'm too busy. I'm too weak. I have other responsibilities." Do you know what combats every one of those excuses? God simply reminds the excuse-maker of Himself. "I am what is good and necessary. I am with you. I am first." He did that with Moses too. Are you seeing the pattern yet? God isn't in the business of stroking our egos. Instead, God points our excuse-making, dream-doubting selves to Him over and over again. This sense of dependency is what motivates us toward action and success.

As we trust God as our Redeemer, our priorities change. We don't need to please people as much. Our identity isn't based on our job titles, salaries, or performance. Anxiety takes a back seat as we realize the weight of the world doesn't ride on us. Continue to trust the One who is calling you, not the thing you're called to. Christ will carry you through for His glory and the good of others!

## Talk to God About This

Are you embracing your excuses or clinging to Christ?

## Simple Prayer

Lord, I'm sorry for the times I've rejected You!
Empower me to embrace Your will. Amen.

# The Next Best Adventure Step

○  Phew! No more excuses. To start doing, go to the next chapter and keep reading.

○  Want to break down the dream before you have a breakdown? Read chapter 25, and then come back here to pick up where you left off.

*Don't forget to check off day 15 as complete on the contents page.*

| My Excuse | God's Assurance |
|---|---|
| "I'm a nobody." | "I will be with you" (see Exodus 3:11-12). |
| "I don't know enough." | "I AM WHO I AM" (see Exodus 3:13-15). |
| "I don't think they'll believe me." | "My presence provides" (see Exodus 4:1-5). |
| "I'm not talented enough." | "I will guide you" (see Exodus 4:10-12). |
| "I don't want to do it." | "I will contribute" (see Exodus 4:13-17). |
| "I am too busy." | "I am what is good and necessary" (see Luke 10:38-42). |
| "I thought it would be different." | "I am God" (see 2 Kings 5:1-15). |
| "I don't understand." | "Trust in Me, not you" (see Proverbs 3:5). |
| "I am too young." | "Do not be afraid, I am with you" (see Jeremiah 1:4-8). |
| "I am too old." | "Nothing is too hard for Me" (see Genesis 18:9-15). |

| My Excuse | God's Assurance |
|---|---|
| "I might suffer." | "I also suffered" (see 1 Peter 3:13-20). |
| "I am weak." | "I am with you" (see Judges 6:15-16). |
| | "My grace is sufficient for you" (see 2 Corinthians 12:7-10). |
| "I need to focus on other responsibilities, like my family." | "I am first. Blessed is everyone who will eat bread in the kingdom of God" (see Luke 14:15-33). |
| | "Follow Me" (see Luke 9:59-62). |
| "I am afraid." | "Be strong and courageous. I am with you. I go before you. I will not leave or forsake you. Do not fear" (see Deuteronomy 31:6-8). |
| | "Fear not for I am with you; do not be dismayed, for I am your God. I will strengthen you, help you and uphold you with my righteous right hand" (see Isaiah 41:10). |
| | "I am the Lord your God, and I hold your right hand. I am the one who tells you, 'Fear not.' I am the one who helps you" (see Isaiah 41:13). |
| | "I am your light and salvation. I am your stronghold" (see Psalm 27:1). |
| | "I will fight for you" (see Deuteronomy 3:22). |

# TAKE ACTION TOWARD YOUR CALL AND INFLUENCE OTHERS FOR CHRIST.

# Act 3

## Stop Daydreaming
## and Start Doing

# 16

# INTRODUCTION TO ACT 3

*Our goals can only be reached through a vehicle of a plan,*
*in which we must fervently believe, and upon which we*
*must vigorously act. There is no other route to success.*

PABLO PICASSO

If a family were a corporation, a parent's title might be Director of Little Humans. The kids may call it being bossy, but we grown-ups know we're training them to some-day thrive and have fun as fully functioning adults who love Jesus.

The Director of Little Humans' job description includes handing out a lot of reminders. "Brush your teeth." "Put your homework in your schoolbag." "If you really want to go sledding off the roof, for the love of all things holy, please wear a helmet and some shin guards."

Of course, the little humans get to respond however they want—ignore us, ask questions, go kicking and screaming, happily follow as we lead—but their decisions bring consequences. If the little humans brush their teeth, they reap the blessings. If they don't, their oral health suffers. So does their social life. Who wants to be nick-named "Stank Breath"?

Parents ask their children to follow their lead, and God is asking His children to do the same. The difference is that He's the Director of All the Things and is lead-ing humanity to Himself. It feels like there's a lot of *umph* behind His directing, don't ya think? I'm glad He's gracious and kind with my whiny little dream-achieving self.

Working from home as you tackle that to-do list dreams are made of? Change out of your jammies, brush your hair, and put that game face on. This will help you show up fresh. Bonus points if you show up fancy or fun in your wedding attire or ninja costume. Yes, I'm speaking from experience.

It's time to trust the One who's calling you, not the thing you're called to. I hope the first two acts of this book have helped you develop a fresh understanding of how God invites us to dream. God brings freedom as He helps you process hard questions and adjust your mindset. Now it's time to respond.

God is asking you to do something significant in this season of life. He isn't playing Mr. Bossy Pants; He's loving you as your Father. From small goals to big ones, He's speaking to you and inviting you to discover the method behind His mission. Like the little humans, you get to decide how you'll respond.

Act 3, the last section of this book, will help you work through the practical tasks that can bring your dream to life. From implementing accountability to goal setting, let's be transformed from dreamers into doers. Put that pen to paper—we've got some work to do as God brings His purpose to pass. It's time to take action toward your call and influence others for Christ.

May we pray this Scripture with the same conviction Paul had as he wrote to the Thessalonian church:

> To this end we always pray for you, that our God may make you worthy of his calling and may fulfill every resolve for good and every work of faith by his power, so that the name of our Lord Jesus may be glorified in you, and you in him, according to the grace of our God and the Lord Jesus Christ (2 Thessalonians 1:11-12).

*Simple Prayer*

Lord, I'm ready to respond to Your call. Amen.

# The Next Best Adventure Step

○ Let's start by pinpointing your passions. Turn the page and keep reading.

○ If you've already completed chapter 17, go to the next unread chapter.

*Don't forget to check off day 16 as complete on the contents page.*

# 17

# LOOKING BACK TO SEE WHAT'S AHEAD

*Lovely One, if you dare to dream, you
must be brave enough to fight.*

LISA BEVERE

If you look at the trajectory of Moses's life, you see his passion for his people. Obstacles stood in the way of that passion even before God revealed his calling to free the Israelites. We will face barriers in our own lives too, but we can remain confident that God has commissioned us and is empowering us to work with Him. And like Moses, we can see our passions as key indicators of what He may be calling us to do.

## Questions to Help You Identify Your Passions

- Are you facing any obstacles in life?
- If yes, are the obstacles caused by your passions?
- What makes you angry?
- What do you get excited about?
- What keeps you up at night?
- What do you enjoy doing for fun?
- Where and with whom do you like to spend your time?
- What do you look forward to?
- What did you love to do as a child?

We get to work and play for the glory of God and good of others. The passions associated with our pleasure and play provide great opportunities to connect with other people and enjoy God through various hobbies and moments of relaxation. Are any of your passions "holy pain points"? They may reveal a more intimate work God is doing in and through your life. Each one matters and can play a significant part in uncovering and advancing the dream God is inviting you to pursue in this season. Spend about 20 minutes working through the Call to Action on page 90.

## Simple Prayer

Lord, may I glorify and enjoy You as You use my passions to push me forward. Amen.

## The Next Best Adventure Step

○ If you jumped here from chapter 3, turn back to chapter 4 to pick up where you left off.

○ Ready to face the dream? Turn to chapter 18 and keep reading. If you've already completed chapter 18, go to the next unread chapter.

*Don't forget to check off day 17 as complete on the contents page.*

## *Call to* ACTION
### List Your Passions

Ask God to highlight your interests, hobbies, and passion points from childhood to now. Write them all down and check the appropriate box.

| PASSION | PLEASURE / PLAY | HOLY PAIN POINT |
|---|:---:|:---:|
| *Playing basketball on Saturday mornings with friends* | ☑ | ☐ |
| *Advocating for clean water for villages in Kenya* | ☐ | ☑ |
| _____ | ☐ | ☐ |
| _____ | ☐ | ☐ |
| _____ | ☐ | ☐ |
| _____ | ☐ | ☐ |
| _____ | ☐ | ☐ |
| _____ | ☐ | ☐ |
| _____ | ☐ | ☐ |
| _____ | ☐ | ☐ |
| _____ | ☐ | ☐ |
| _____ | ☐ | ☐ |
| _____ | ☐ | ☐ |
| _____ | ☐ | ☐ |
| _____ | ☐ | ☐ |
| _____ | ☐ | ☐ |

After you prayerfully work through your passions, star or highlight the ones you feel God is prioritizing in this right-now season.

# 18

# HELLO, DREAM, I SEE YOU

*A primary qualification for serving God with any
amount of success, and for doing God's work well and
triumphantly, is a sense of our own weakness.*

CHARLES HADDON SPURGEON

The Bible shares a grace-filled moment when Isaiah, a Hebrew man, received a vision from God. As he stood in the Lord's presence, he was overwhelmed with God's holiness and his own unworthiness, and he responded with heartfelt repentance.

> In the year that King Uzziah died I saw the Lord sitting upon a throne, high and lifted up; and the train of his robe filled the temple. Above him stood the seraphim. Each had six wings: with two he covered his face, and with two he covered his feet, and with two he flew. And one called to another and said:
>
> "Holy, holy, holy is the LORD of hosts;
> the whole earth is full of his glory!"
>
> And the foundations of the thresholds shook at the voice of him who called, and the house was filled with smoke. And I said: "Woe is me! For I am lost; for I am a man of unclean lips, and I dwell in the midst of a people of unclean lips; for my eyes have seen the King, the LORD of hosts!"
>
> Then one of the seraphim flew to me, having in his hand a burning coal that he had taken with tongs from the altar. And he touched my mouth and

> said: "Behold, this has touched your lips; your guilt is taken away, and your sin atoned for."
>
> And I heard the voice of the Lord saying, "Whom shall I send, and who will go for us?" Then I said, "Here I am! Send me" (Isaiah 6:1-8).

Humility helps us say hello to the call of God. The Christian dream isn't built on the American dream; it starts with dependence on God! This becomes the birth-place of courage. That's why it's so important to recognize God's voice, understand His invitation, and respond appropriately.

Perhaps your dream doesn't feel as big as Isaiah's or Moses's. I want to remind you that God's everyday call is just as significant as the "extravagant" ones. When God invited you to go talk to your neighbor, did you go? What about that friend who's in crisis and has been praying for help? God may answer that prayer by encour-aging you to be a friend who listens, prays, and supports.

On the other hand, maybe you feel like you're going to puke your guts out because your dream seems so big and scary.

Either way, now is your time, dreamer. Are you ready to make it official? Answer God's call:

Here I am! Send me.

☐ Yes!                    ☐ No way!

(Read chapter 32.)

## Sometimes in Life You Have to Be Courageous

One fall day in 2017, I was in New York City with some friends. We had just eaten dinner and were sitting at a cupcake shop when our phones began buzzing. Mes-sage after message poured in from friends asking if we were okay. We found out a small bomb had detonated not far from where we were. Feeling scared, we ditched the cupcakes and decided to head back to our hotel, which was about an hour out-side the city. Seeking safety, we hailed a taxi and asked the driver to take us to the train station.

Unfortunately, everyone else had the same idea. We sat motionless in bumper-to-bumper traffic. The driver turned on the radio—the bomb had made the news, and there were concerns of more. As my friends and I talked about this tragedy, we mentioned September 11, 2001.

It turns out our driver saw the attack on the Twin Towers. He watched as the second tower crumbled to the ground. He began sharing his heart with us three girls smushed in the back of his cab, reliving one of the most challenging days of his life. We sat still, silently wondering if we were facing another attack.

Suddenly, our driver decided we had waited long enough. "Hold on!" he yelled. With ninja-like moves, he pulled out of the traffic surrounding us and created his own route at what felt like 100 miles an hour. I didn't know this was possible, but we almost got rear-ended, broadsided, and hit head-on all at once.

He continued to drive like a maniac. I closed my eyes, thinking if I couldn't see this wild rollercoaster ride, it wasn't really happening. But it was, and I was pretty sure I was going to die. So I screamed, "What are you doing!"

Without missing a beat, he yelled back, "Sometimes in life you have to be courageous!"

Our screams of fear turned into wild cheers. We praised his driving all the way to safety. Something shifted for us when we realized the cab driver was working for our good. It was almost as if he wanted our safety more than we did. Was it a super uncomfortable process? Yes. But here's the thing...

So is dreaming. It can be uncomfortable and messy. We can feel gridlocked or under attack. What does it take to shift your perspective? How can you stop screaming in fear and start to cheer?

It all depends on your perspective, on remembering that God is with you as you pursue His dreams for you. That He wants what is best for you. And for those reasons, sometimes in life you have to be courageous.

## Why Writing Down Dreams Matters

Neuropsychologists have done studies showing how important it is to write stuff down. A Forbes article shares, "Writing things down happens on two levels: external storage and encoding." As you write down your goal or dream, you're externally storing it. If you put it in a prominent place, you'll be reminded of your goal daily. Then there's encoding.

Encoding is the biological process by which the things we perceive travel to our brain's hippocampus where they're analyzed. From there, decisions are made about what gets stored in our long-term memory and, in turn, what gets discarded. Writing improves that encoding process. In other words, when you write it down it has a much greater chance of being remembered.[1]

## *Call to* ACTION
### Say Hello to the Dream and See It Often

Write down that one big dream you're committed to pursuing in this right-now season. Make a note of it in your Divine Strategic Plan on page 47.

After you write down your dream, take it a step further and set an alarm on your phone that will buzz and remind you of it daily. Or write it on a piece of paper and put it in a place you'll see often. Let me be clear: You're not writing it down to "manifest your miracle" because you saw your self-help sticky note. Writing it down will serve as reminder of the work God has done and is doing in your life. It's a piece of perspective. It will also be a reminder of the courageous work you do as you move forward in obedience.

Sometimes we have to become discontent before we will demonstrate courage. If we are content to leave our God-sized dream on the shelf, we might never take any action on it even though God is placing value on it. But when we are reminded of our dream every day, we might not be so happy ignoring it. We might pray about it more or talk about it with a supportive friend who might ask the hard questions. We might even become dissatisfied with the status quo. *This is good!* Because when we don't want to continue avoiding our God-dream any longer, we might finally find the courage to take action. And it can start by placing that dream in the forefront of our minds and hearts daily. Externally storing and internally encoding God's dream for the right-now season is imperative to remaining courageous.

## Simple Prayer

Lord, give me Your words to write and dream! Amen.

## The Next Best Adventure Step

○  If you jumped here from chapter 4, turn back to chapter 5 to pick up where you left off.

○  Is right now the time to pursue this dream? Turn the page and keep reading to find out. If you've already completed chapter 19, go to the next unread chapter.

*Don't forget to check off day 18 as complete on the contents page.*

# 19

## THE RIGHT SEASON

*The call of God is not just for a select few but for everyone.*
*Whether I hear God's call or not depends on the condition of my*
*ears, and exactly what I hear depends upon my spiritual attitude.*

OSWALD CHAMBERS

Imagine putting on a bathing suit and stepping outside into a blizzard. Or bundling up in your puffer coat but opening the door to 90-degree weather. You're in the wrong season!

As you embrace your dream, don't force it to happen if it isn't the right time. Being out of season can make you really uncomfortable. God wants to choose when and where you make a move toward His dream for you. So in this chapter, we're going to talk about focusing on the right-now season.

As the apostle Paul began fulfilling his calling to preach the gospel, the Lord moved through him to strengthen and grow the church. Paul understood the vision and followed God's leading. Miracles, healings, and salvations were happening as God ministered through Paul. Yet Paul knew he wasn't the author of this story. In fact, as Paul was traveling, the Holy Spirit halted Paul's plans—twice.

> Paul and his companions traveled throughout the region of Phrygia and Galatia, having been kept by the Holy Spirit from preaching the word in the province of Asia. When they came to the border of Mysia, they tried to enter Bithynia, but the Spirit of Jesus would not allow them to. So they passed by Mysia and went down to Troas (Acts 16:6-8 NIV).

*Four years later*, Paul took his disciples and shared the word of the Lord in the province of Asia (Acts 19:10).[1] He may have wondered if he'd ever minister in Asia, but he remained attentive to where the Lord was leading—it just looked different from his own plan. Paul couldn't be in two places at once, and God prioritized where he would go and when.

Finally embracing a dream from God is awesome, but it doesn't mean you get to stop talking to Him about it! One of the joys of having a relationship with God is that we get to continue a two-way dialogue with Him. He wants to use that dialogue to provide us with resources, comfort, and guidance from the Holy Spirit.

Is right now the season for your one big dream? Have you asked Him? God is responding with one of three things:

"No."

"Go."

"Whoaahhh, not yet." (Imagine Him tugging on your reins.)

## *Call to* ACTION
### Did God Say Go?

These seven questions are from my book *Getting to Know God's Voice*.[2] They can help you determine whether your dream is in season. Let these key questions guide you as you prayerfully consider if God is saying, "Go!"

1. Does what I am considering agree with Scripture?
2. Will this situation bring me closer to God?
3. What do my spiritual leaders think about this situation?
4. What is the still, small voice of God saying to me?
5. What circumstances are surrounding this situation?
6. What do my trusted friends and family say about this?
7. What response will bring peace?

How do you feel God is leading?

☐ No    ☐ Go    ☐ Whoaahhh, not yet.

None of God's responses is more holy than the others. You're living "faith for-ward" as you hear His direction and trust His timing. Paying attention to God's clock brings comfort, even when that dream makes you feel uncomfortable.

As we saw in Paul's experience, some goals can take years to come into fruition. But Paul held on to the vision and made himself available to serve regardless of the path God was leading him on. In the same way, even if this isn't the right season for you to reach a particular goal, you can continue to participate in God's unfolding story.

As you continue working through this book, try not to wear your bathing suit in the snow. Beware of creating your own seasons because you think you need to per-form well or please other people. In this season, God may be producing patience in you, positioning you, or propelling you toward that God-given dream. Trust His tim-ing...God flips the calendar as He sees fit. As you follow His lead, you can be sure you're in the right season.

## Simple Prayer

Lord, may I hear Your "yes," "no," or
"whoaahhh!" loud and clear. Amen.

## The Next Best Adventure Step

○ If you jumped here from chapter 7, turn back to chapter 8 to pick up where you left off.

○ Who do you dream for? Turn the page and keep reading to find out. If you've already completed chapter 20, go to the next unread chapter.

*Don't forget to check off day 19 as complete on the contents page.*

# 20

# KNOW YOUR ~~WHY~~ WHO

*A merchant who approaches business with the idea of serving
the public well has nothing to fear from the competition.*

JAMES CASH PENNEY

As author and leadership expert Simon Sinek spoke, he drew three concentric circles on a giant piece of paper with the word "why" in the center. This has become one of the most popular talks given from the Ted Talk stage, with more than fifty million views. Simon taught that to be an excellent leader and to motivate action, you must understand your why. This idea went on to inspire marketing campaigns, promote business growth, and further individual leadership development. Identifying the why behind your goals or aspirations will sharpen your focus and point you down the right path to achieve that thing.[1]

I understand the power behind this exercise. In fact, we've used it to strengthen our creative agency. But let's take it a step further. What drives you to pursue your dream? Behind the "why" stands the "who." As Paul shares with the churches in Galatia, "You, my brothers and sisters, were called to be free. But do not use your freedom to indulge the flesh; rather, serve one another humbly in love (Galatians 5:13 NIV). Jesus said something similar in the Great Commandment:

> "Love the Lord your God with all your heart and with all your soul and with all your mind." This is the first and greatest commandment. And the second is

99

like it: "Love your neighbor as yourself." All the Law and the Prophets hang on these two commandments (Matthew 22:37-40 NIV).

Clearly identifying who your goal serves (your target audience) is key to knowing how to serve them well. As we have seen, our dream ultimately brings glory to God. But how do you discover the other "who"—your target audience?

As part of your process of identifying your target audience, try creating fictional characters, or avatars. The more detailed this fictional profile is, the easier it will be to understand who you're reaching. This helps you develop consistent language, assess your audience's needs, and understand their struggles. You can then cater your plan to their pain points and create and communicate in a way that best supports them.

> ## INSTEAD OF THE *WHY* MOTIVATING US TO SHOW UP, WHAT IF OUR FOCUS WAS SIMPLY *WHO*?

For example, in writing my book *Courageous Creative*, I was motivated to develop two avatars for my readers. I combed through magazines and created a collage of two audiences.

- Jim is a young professional who compartmentalized his creative gifts and talents. His dad told him art wasn't a job, and now he feels he was forced to pursue a traditional desk job to earn a living. What does it take to get Jim to embrace his God-given creativity and step into his full potential?

- Joy, 37, is a professional creative who needs to overcome creativity killers like people-pleasing and perfectionism. She's desperate to gain greater freedom, and she's willing to learn through trial and error and take some risks. What does it take to get Joy to elevate her creative expression to become a leader in her work environment?

I used these avatars as jumping-off points for research and content development in *Courageous Creative*. I gave both avatars real names, wrote out specific demographics, created collages of their imaginary lives, and hung their profiles by my desk. Years later I'm still hearing from people who fit into my fictional avatars' stories. Because of that, the real-life Jims and Joys are finding freedom of expression through my book.

My big dream of writing a book on creativity wasn't based on my abilities but on loving those around me. Clearly identifying the "who" keeps the focus off you. And there's an added bonus to this mindset: When you fail (and you will), you won't have an identity crisis, because the dream isn't about you anyway. You're showing up because of who you're serving and Who has called you.

At the end of this chapter you'll find a target audience tool kit to help you identify who your dream benefits. Here are some key thoughts before you take action in the next section.

- If you think your dream will impact everyone, I invite you to niche down as much as possible. Yes, your reach may extend beyond your avatars, but prayerfully considering the "who" in greater detail will help you communicate to that audience powerfully and effectively.

- Perhaps you are already reaching people. Keep them in mind as examples as you fill out the toolkit.

- Don't force your "who" to fit into every category.

- Your dream may serve multiple audiences of people.

Remember, your dream is for the glory of God and the good of others! After all, *God is glorified when we spread His goodness to others.* Enjoy this process of thinking about the people God could reach through your work. Lives will be seen, supported, and transformed as you dream big with God.

## Simple Prayer

Lord, bring me clear wisdom on who You're inviting
me to serve with this dream. Amen.

# The Next Best Adventure Step

After you work through the tool kit, take the next step...

- ○ If you jumped here from chapter 5, turn back to chapter 6 to pick up where you left off.

- ○ Read chapter 21 and phone a friend. If you've already completed chapter 21, go to the next unread chapter.

*Don't forget to check off day 20 as complete on the contents page.*

# *Call to* ACTION
## The Target Audience Tool Kit

Who is God inviting you to impact? Develop your dream by describing the "who."

| Name | Age | Gender | Marital Status | Children's ages |
|------|-----|--------|----------------|-----------------|
|      |     |        |                |                 |

| Location | Education |
|----------|-----------|
|          |           |

| Employer | Job Title |
|----------|-----------|
|          |           |

| Income Level | Lifestyle |
|--------------|-----------|
|              |           |

| Personality Traits | Values and Beliefs |
|--------------------|--------------------|
|                    |                    |

Interests (TV shows, books, podcasts, conferences...)

Hobbies (sports, arts, outdoors, cooking...)

Favorite hangouts (online and in person)

Frustrations and fears

Challenges

Goals

# 21

# IMPLEMENTING ACCOUNTABILITY, AND THE TEXTS THAT WILL HAUNT YOU

*Accountability separates the wishers in life from the action-takers that care enough about their future to account for their daily actions.*

JOHN DI LEMME

"Did you write those words today?" The simple text on my phone buzzed as I shoved ice cream in my face and watched *Napoleon Dynamite* for the umpteenth time.

I wanted to respond with a sassy quote from the movie. "I don't even have any good skills. You know, like nunchuck skills, bow-hunting skills, computer hacking skills." But instead, I turned off the movie, opened up my computer, and replied, "Nah, was feeling like a lazy lady but am starting right now. Thanks for checking and holding me to it!"

Months earlier, I asked two accountability partners to ask me once a week if I was writing. They asked me specific follow-up questions like these:

- "Where does writing fit into your schedule?" To which I promptly responded, "At night, after the kids go to bed."

- "How often during the week will you be writing?" Answer: "Every weeknight."

Yet there I sat for the third day in a row, ignoring my verbal commitments to God, myself, my friends, and my calendar. The text was just the gut punch of encouragement I needed. God has used different forms of accountability to empower me to finish my books, host sunrise prayer at an ungodly hour (turns out it's way more godly than I had anticipated), and reset my workaholic tendencies. Accountability helped me establish creative disciplines, create rhythms, and replace some unhealthy habits.

My accountability partners understood how this dream to write fit into my life and kindly called me out when they saw me shrinking back from pursuing it. They were also praying for the project, and they were first ones in line to buy the book. They not only called me *out* but also called me *up*.

> Dear brothers and sisters, if another believer is overcome by some sin, you who are godly should gently and humbly help that person back onto the right path. And be careful not to fall into the same temptation yourself. Share each other's burdens, and in this way obey the law of Christ. If you think you are too important to help someone, you are only fooling yourself. You are not that important.
>
> Pay careful attention to your own work, for then you will get the satisfaction of a job well done, and you won't need to compare yourself to anyone else. For we are each responsible for our own conduct (Galatians 6:1-5 NLT).

The next call to action will help you build accountability into your work. Communicating expectations up front helps me stay focused on what I feel called to do. It also keeps accountability from turning into a cluster of complaints. Here are some do's and don'ts of accountability you may find helpful:

## ACCOUNTABILITY SHOULDN'T SUCK THE LIFE OUT OF SOMEONE; IT BREATHES LIFE INTO THEM, EMPOWERING THEM TO SHOW UP.

- You aren't asking people to carry your vision, do the work for you, or hold your hand as you dot every *i*.
- They aren't there to stroke your ego or validate your purpose. Rather, they are there to ask hard questions to help you eliminate excuses so you can follow through on your commitments.

- Establishing accountability is one of the best ways to stay focused, place value on your dream, and accomplish your goal.

Some accountability partners may be so all-in, they will help you evaluate your process and will mark your due dates on their own calendars. Accountability takes you off an island of isolation and reminds you that you're not in this alone. As you share your dream with trusted friends or family members, continue to remain humble and honest. Vulnerability coupled with action leads to transformation!

## Simple Prayer

Lord, thank You for the gift of accountability. Amen.

## The Next Best Adventure Step

After you complete the call to action, take the next step...

- If you jumped here from chapter 9, turn back to chapter 10 to pick up where you left off.

- Turn to chapter 22 and keep reading to get in position to achieve your goals. If you've already completed chapter 22, go to the next unread chapter.

*Don't forget to check off day 21 as complete on the contents page.*

# *Call to* ACTION
## Implement Accountability

1. List several trusted friends, family members, or colleagues with whom you share a mutually beneficial relationship.

_____   _____

_____   _____

_____   _____

_____

Prayerfully ask God to highlight two or three names on your list. Circle those names.

2. Right now, drop them a text or email, or give them a call. Keep it casual. Here are some words you can use if you like:

> Hey [insert name], I feel like God is inviting me to pursue [insert dream]. I've seen how valuable holding one another accountable can be in the process of goal setting. I was wondering if you'd be interested in holding me accountable to finishing? I value your friendship and feel like I can be honest with you throughout the process. Just a simple check-in text from time to time would help me maintain momentum. If you're available, let me know, and I'll tell you my due dates. You'll have full permission to call me out if I start procrastinating. Your support in this would mean the world to me! And if there's ever anything I can do to support and help champion you, let me know!

Did you do it?

☐ Yes            ☐ No

Once you receive the responses, list the accountability partners who will help you pursue your dream:

_____        _____

_____        _____

_____        _____

# 22

# POSITIONING YOURSELF TO ACHIEVE YOUR GOALS

*Practice is the hardest part of learning, and*
*training is the essence of transformation.*

ANN VOSKAMP

I came face to face with my first divine pivot point in third grade. My teacher was watching the "film" I wrote and produced. Seeing her connect to a project I had created ignited something in my spirit. God used this kindling to spark so many dreams and adventures. I DJed on a radio station that reached a neighborhood block, I developed a local TV show...and these moments marked me. When I became a Christ-follower, my passion to glorify and enjoy Him was woven into my creative expression.

As my age and faith increased, the vision did too. I dreamed of working professionally as a video editor in the entertainment industry. After graduating from college with a degree in television (yes, that's a thing), I realized I couldn't pursue that dream from where I lived in the suburbs of Upstate New York. After God established His divine strategic plan for this career goal, I positioned myself for the new season. I moved to Los Angeles, where dreamers pitch their emerging skill sets and million-dollar scripts at gas stations, traffic lights, and taco bars.

I soon landed a job with a post-production company working as a receptionist. Dreams hardly ever start at the top. I answered phones, ordered lunches, and figured out how to make coffee. For years I honored and served the dreams of others while stewarding and strengthening the vision God had given me. After hours, my boss let me use the industry-standard equipment to develop my editing skills. I volunteered to edit my local church's small-group curriculum and continued to position myself to reach my professional goals. I didn't feel like I was striving to achieve; instead, I felt like I was living out a divine strategy.

Sometimes God's path toward that one big thing includes lots of practice steps. Many dreamers think their seasons of apprenticeship are irrelevant, so the time is wasted. Don't be so distracted by your dream that you miss the growth opportunity right in front of you. You cannot lead until you learn to follow.

Whether you are in a season of preparation or celebrating your accomplishments, God is worthy to be praised. Your position doesn't propel you forward; God does. These defining moments in your God-sized adventure may contribute to your identity, but they don't dictate your worth. It's God's story, remember?

When God called the apostle Paul to spread the gospel, Paul didn't sit still in Antioch. God instructed Paul on the go. Your God-dream may be larger than your current setting, and sometimes you have to move to see it fulfilled. You may have a dream that requires you to network,

**REMAINING PASSIVE WHEN GOD IS INVITING YOU TO TAKE ACTION DEMONSTRATES DISOBEDIENCE.**

take start-up opportunities, get a degree, adjust your schedule, or relocate.

When you position yourself to achieve your goal, you aren't usurping God's authority. Rather, you're cooperating with it. Use the following call to action to unpack these thoughts. Take your time on this and dive in.

## Simple Prayer

Lord, show me how You're inviting me to move. Amen.

# The Next Best Adventure Step

After you complete the call to action on the next page, take the next step...

○ If you jumped here from chapter 13, turn back to chapter 14 to pick up where you left off.

○ Unwrap your gifts in chapter 23. If you've already completed chapter 23, go to the next unread chapter.

*Don't forget to check off day 22 as complete on the contents page.*

# *Call to* ACTION
## Get in Position

Take the next twenty minutes to prayerfully brain dump and word vomit. (Yes, it's just as fun as I just described it.) It may feel messy and uncomfortable. In the middle of the space below, summarize your dream in a few words. Then draw a mind map—a graphic list of the areas in which God may be inviting you to reposition yourself to pursue your dream.

Over the next few days, pray over this list. Grab a highlighter and mark any areas in which God may be asking you to take a step. Run your thoughts by your accountability partner, trusted friends, or pastoral support to gauge their thoughts. If it's a big move, use discernment and confirm that you're hearing God's voice. Take action as He leads. Note any goals that are here to stay on page 48 (the Divine Strategic Plan). I'll be over here throwing confetti and cheering you on as you show up in the uncomfortability of all this!

# 23

# THE TALENTED AND GIFTED PROGRAM

*Career should be a spiritual pursuit, not just a physical or financial*
*one. Your career should be where your dreams, aspirations,*
*talents, and hopes for the present and future play out.*

DEVON FRANKLIN

You may be using your talents and God-given abilities to design graphics for local businesses in town. Maybe you can engineer mechanical gadgets faster than most people can do simple arithmetic. Perhaps your prophetic gifting helps people to feel seen and loved. One way or another, God has given you natural and supernatural abilities, and the rest of us need you to put them to good use as you pursue your dream.

> As each has received a gift, use it to serve one another, as good stewards of God's varied grace: whoever speaks, as one who speaks oracles of God; whoever serves, as one who serves by the strength that God supplies—in order that in everything God may be glorified through Jesus Christ. To him belong glory and dominion forever and ever. Amen (1 Peter 4:10-11).

## Why We Acknowledge Our Gifts

Circle the word "gift" in 1 Peter 4:10 above. The Greek word for "gift" translates to the English word "charisma." Charisma refers to something graciously given. In the New Testament, charisma is closely connected to grace and favor. God is the one who gives these types of gifts, including spiritual gifts for equipping the church (1 Corinthians 12:4), a person's special calling (2 Timothy 1:6), and God's gift of salvation through Christ (Romans 5:15-16; 6:23; 11:29). As you can see, a gift is the consequence of gracious giving or action.[1]

In nonreligious contexts, "charisma" simply refers to a person's charm or appeal. But the word's etymology reminds us that when we say, "That person has charisma," we're recognizing the favor and grace God has supplied them.

When we acknowledge our own gifting, we're telling God, "Okay, I see You, and I receive what You've given me." On the other hand, if we downplay our talents or giftings, aren't we actually doubting God? I don't want to get to the end of my life and reflect on the gifts I disregarded or rejected out of fear of being too much or not enough. I want to glorify God, the Giver of my gift to communicate, as I boldly stand on a stage to preach, knowing full well He put me there. I want my son to honor God by appreciating his wizard-like math skills. I want you to boldly and bravely hold your hands out to receive the talents and gifts God is handing you. As you do, you're courageously embracing Him. You're trusting the Gift giver. When we steward our dreams well, we open the gifts God has given us and use them as He intended.

Look at the following call to action and work through the questions. You'll end up with a list of your God-given talents, gifts, and abilities that will help you achieve your dream.

Call to ACTION
The Gift List

What natural and supernatural talents has God given you?

What qualities do people notice about you?

In what areas do others look to you as an expert?

Have you taken a personality assessment and spiritual gifts test?
If so, what did you learn?

## Why We Don't Make Idols of Our Gifts

By God's grace, your gift list is different from others'. After all, God knows you intimately, so of course He would know how to give you a gift. God's favor separates you from the crowd. It's important to understand your unique gifts and to see them as valuable. However, even this shouldn't define you or become an idol. When our gift lists become more important than triune God (Father, Son, Holy Spirit), we're worshipping the wrong things.

Yes, you're awesome. Yes, let's acknowledge God's favor through the gifts He's given. Yes, let's serve from the strength and courage God provides.

But let's acknowledge God for who He is *more* than the things He's given. He gives us amazing things that are rooted in His grace and love. I'm reminded of my middle-school boyfriend, who would pay for my movie ticket every time we went on a date. Until one day, he didn't. I expected a free pass because of our relationship, so I hadn't brought any money with me. Things got awkward real fast as I mumbled my way through *my* expectations.

When someone's nature is to habitually care for us and love us, we can begin to feel entitled, as if we're owed something. There really is more substance to our relationship with God than just getting great stuff from Him. If God's grace truly is sufficient, isn't He enough? Let's not chase our dream the way we're chasing Christ. As we read in 1 Peter 4:11, God gets the glory in everything—in our dreams, in our gifts, and even in our beating heart. And trust me on this: There is more joy to be found in the things that glorify God than in the things that glorify us!

Now turn to that gift list again. Before it gets to your head, scribble it out. Seriously, do it. Talent may turn a room, but God is the one who elevates you. Don't build your life on your abilities or charm. We must remain humble as we use our gifts to help others. Romans 12:3 says, "By the grace given to me I say to everyone among you not to think of himself more highly than he ought to think, but to think with sober judgment, each according to the measure of faith that God has assigned."

With or without Christ, you may be able to build your own kingdom of wealth and fame. But how much greater is the privilege and honor of building His kingdom! As we seek God's glory and not our ego and agenda, we build intimacy with our Father. So look to Christ—not just for support and strengthening but as your lifeline.

Did you scribble out that list? Regardless of how talented you are, you can't experience God's dream for you without Him. As you continue to walk out this dream, remember that Christ is the one who is carrying you.

## Simple Prayer

Lord, may I humbly use my gifts for Your glory
and the good of others. Amen.

## The Next Best Adventure Step

○ Did you get here from chapter 2? Turn back to chapter 3 to pick up where you left off.

○ Want to check out your tool belt? Turn the page and keep reading. If you've already completed chapter 24, go to the next unread chapter.

*Don't forget to check off day 23 as complete on the contents page.*

# 24

# TRAINING AND TOOLS

*Preparation, I have often said, is rightly two-thirds of any venture.*
AMELIA EARHART

During my junior year of college, some of my classmates and I moved from New York to Los Angeles to intern for a semester. In addition to working at daytime television shows and studios and visiting film sets, we loved exploring the town. It was quickly living up to its glamorous "city of dreams" nickname...for most of us.

"What's your dream in life?" I asked my friend who also majored in television and was looking for work in the entertainment industry. His response had me laughing out loud and sizing him up big-time:

"I want to be a professional basketball player," he responded with childlike wonder.

I wondered if he was semi-delusional and wasting his money on a private school education. He was getting hands-on training to make shows with the stars, not to become a basketball all-star. So Buzzkill Jenny responded, "Dreaming takes you only so far. Why haven't you been in training to be a pro basketball player? Do you even own a ball?"

He was average height with an overweight bod. He resembled a pro athlete about as much as an anthill resembles Mountain Everest. And boy, did Slacker have some mountains to climb to compete in the NBA. He hadn't played basketball since middle school. His lifelong dream felt way out of bounds to me.

Typically, I'm in the front row crying happy tears and throwing confetti as I cheer on the dreamers. But not this time. I don't mean to be all judgmental, but this reminded me of the popular verse "I can do whatever I stinking want through Christ who gives me strength." (I'm paraphrasing of course.)

I once wished to be a professional singer with pipes like Christina Aguilera. But even though this tone-deaf girl wanted to be a pop star, I never attempted a voice lesson. I finally realized, "No, I can't do whatever I want." And we can't take Bible verses out of context and act like God is our free pass to success.

Dreamers should have their heads in the stars and their sneakers on the ground. Pursuing a new (or shelved) dream requires recognizing your gifts, practicing, and receiving on-the-job training. I genuinely believe you have what it takes to achieve this thing you're setting out to do, so to avoid being an NBA or pop-star wannabe, and to get set up for success, let's think of all the training and tools you may need to achieve it. You don't need to be highly skilled to begin; you just need to be proactive! You can find a wealth of free tutorials, courses, and how-tos online.

Work through the following questions and use your answers to fill in the Dreamer in Training chart at the end of the chapter. Review this chart when you feel stuck in your dream, and get some training. Having these training materials and tools readily available whenever you need to learn more or further develop your talents will help you maintain forward momentum in this God-given dream.

- What software or tools does your dream require?
- Who are the coaches, teachers, leaders, or content creators that can train you (online and in person)?
- What resources can make your training more effective (library, YouTube, internship, books, counseling...)?
- What do you need to learn to pursue this dream? (Example: How does international adoption from China work?)
- Do you need to commit to a training schedule? (Example: Block some time on your calendar to practice using that design software.)

As you put your sneakers to the pavement, you will find plenty of blank spaces between you and God's dream for you. Let Him fill them with resources, tools, talents, equipment, and more. His resources are infinite and limitless. However, His resources come in the context of your relationship with Him. As you get proactive about action items, do not lose sight of what is most important with *any* God-given dream—God Himself. That's why the best tools of all are the ones that cultivate nearness and intimacy with Him.

## YOU DON'T NEED TO BE PERFECT OR A PROFESSIONAL BEFORE BEGINNING, JUST PROACTIVE!

Work through the next call to action to get started. But don't let yourself get stuck in practice mode forever. We practice so we can show up powerfully to see that dream come true.

## Simple Prayer

Lord, help me find the training and tools I need to pursue this dream. Amen.

## The Next Best Adventure Step

After you set up your Dreamer in Training chart, take the next step...

○ Did you get here from chapter 14? Turn back to chapter 15 to pick up where you left off.

○ To break it down before a breakdown, read chapter 25. If you've already completed chapter 25, go to the next unread chapter.

*Don't forget to check off day 24 as complete on the contents page.*

# Call to ACTION
## Dreamer in Training

| SOFTWARE/TOOLS | TRAINING TO ACHIEVE | DATE |
|---|---|---|
| | | |
| | | |
| | | |
| | | |
| | | |

| TEACHERS/COACHES | TRAINING TO ACHIEVE | DATE |
|---|---|---|
| | | |
| | | |
| | | |
| | | |
| | | |

| QUESTIONS | TRAINING TO ACHIEVE | DATE |
|---|---|---|
| | | |
| | | |
| | | |
| | | |

| TRAINING SCHEDULE | TRAINING TO ACHIEVE | DATE |
|---|---|---|
| | | |
| | | |
| | | |
| | | |

*I'm not beneath bribery. My goal is to complete _____ training sessions, and when I do, I get this magical prize:*

# 25

## BREAK IT DOWN BEFORE A BREAKDOWN

*It's essential to draw up a "things to do" list on a daily basis
and set priorities in executing them, making sure that any
unfinished task gets posted to the next day's list.*

FOLORUNSHO ALAKIJA

*Starting a business, writing a book, rebuilding a healthy marriage after an affair...*it's weird how we can have a hope-filled dream but feel weighed down with hopelessness. Big goals can feel overwhelming or overpowering because we don't know how to start. As a result we may simply remain on hold.

Yet Proverbs 16:9 reads, "The heart of man plans his way, but the LORD establishes his steps." Let's see how this worked out in a man named Bezalel.

> The LORD said to Moses, "See, I have called by name Bezalel the son of Uri, son of Hur, of the tribe of Judah, and I have filled him with the Spirit of God, with ability and intelligence, with knowledge and all craftsmanship, to devise artistic designs, to work in gold, silver, and bronze, in cutting stones for setting, and in carving wood, to work in every craft (Exodus 31:1-5).

God gave Bezalel the skill set to be the chief artisan of the tabernacle. God provided vision, gifts, and talents, and He filled Bezalel with His Spirit to complete this build. Bezalel brought God's vision to life as he assigned specific tasks to skilled laborers and began to work through the task list. You can read the specifics in Exodus

36–39. From the tabernacle curtains of goat hair to the ark made of acacia wood, Bezalel oversaw the production of this project.

God is positioning your steps, so it's time to develop a plan. Dr. Gail Matthews, a psychology professor, did a study that showed you are 42 percent more likely to achieve your goals if you write them down. As we learned in chapter 18, writing down your goals cements them into your external storage and encodes them into your long-term memory, which in turn places value on them. And we all know you show up for the things you value. (Hello, pumpkin-spice lattes.)

Here's how to plan out the dream. Turn it into small, actionable items and tasks. Focus on tangible things that you can easily check off. Your to-do list won't seem overwhelming anymore—in fact, it will give you confidence to pursue it. For example, if your goal is to have a healthier marriage, circle which item you feel would be the best actionable task:

- Find a marriage counselor.
- By Friday, ask my pastor for a few local marriage counselor recommendations.

Narrowing in your focus from big, vague, and challenging items to small, specific, and easy-to-manage ones will help you get them done more efficiently and effectively. Use the Macro-to-Micro Task Master at the end of this chapter to become the master of your to-do list in no time. The unachievable, intimidating dream quickly becomes inviting. The path to achieving your dream will emerge as you identify clear and concise tasks. You're breaking down the dream...before you have a breakdown yourself.

As you trust God in this process, you build patience and persistence by pursuing the things He places before you. Maybe today your first step is to make a hard phone call, brainstorm seven ways to raise finances for your nonprofit, or ask your barista friend for that yummy pumpkin-spiced latte recipe.

Break out your pen. Use the Task Master three-step process to increase your productivity:

- Write down your big dream (your macro-level vision).
- List three major tasks that will help you achieve your dream (your major tasks).
- Break each task down into small, actionable items (your micro-level plans).

You're moving from macro-level dreaming to micro-level doing. As you continue to move forward with the dream, repeat the process until the dream comes true. Take the guesswork out of your next best step!

## Simple Prayer

Lord, I need Your macro-level wisdom on how to turn this dream into micro-level doing. Amen.

## The Next Best Adventure Step

After you work through the Task Master...

- ○ Did you get here from chapter 15? Turn back to chapter 16 to pick up where you left off.
- ○ Get out your calendar and read chapter 26.

*Don't forget to check off day 25 as complete on the contents page.*

# Call to ACTION
## The Macro-to-Micro Task Master

**Step 1** Write down your big dream

**Step 2** List three major tasks that will help you achieve your dream

**Step 3** Break each task down into small actionable items

*dream*

1

2

3

- [ ] _____
- [ ] _____
- [ ] _____
- [ ] _____
- [ ] _____
- [ ] _____
- [ ] _____
- [ ] _____
- [ ] _____
- [ ] _____
- [ ] _____

- [ ] _____
- [ ] _____
- [ ] _____
- [ ] _____
- [ ] _____
- [ ] _____
- [ ] _____
- [ ] _____
- [ ] _____
- [ ] _____
- [ ] _____

- [ ] _____
- [ ] _____
- [ ] _____
- [ ] _____
- [ ] _____
- [ ] _____
- [ ] _____
- [ ] _____
- [ ] _____
- [ ] _____
- [ ] _____

*Break it down so you don't have a breakdown!*

# 26

# YOUR CALENDAR IS YOUR BESTIE

*We can say what we want about our priorities, but no
criteria will be as accurate and telling as how we use
our time. Our calendar reflects our true priorities.*

BRAYDEN BROOKSHIER

Today's lesson may be torturous for procrastinators and those who prefer to fly by the seat of their pants. Let's discuss how to manage your schedule honorably so you can steward this dream well. We'll look at some habits you can create to conquer that to-do list and be a highly productive person. Let's touch on a few, and you can google your way through some more to figure out the best task-management system for you. For now, your calendar is your bestie.

What's the best type of calendar for your lifestyle?

☐ Paper        ☐ Digital

## 10 Tips to Managing and Understanding Your Calendar

1. Most likely, there will never be an ideal time to pursue your dream. The only perfect time is God's timing. You may always be busy, but you can reduce feelings of being overwhelmed by reframing your mindset. How? With your words. Instead of saying, "I'm just *so* busy," try saying, "It's a

126

privilege to be able to..." Or "I *get* to...." Stop wearing your busyness as a badge of honor, and remember that *you* are the keeper of your calendar.

2. Use a scheduling system to clarify your process, manage your expectations, and structure your plans. You can create an online calendar or task process, use a paper calendar, or set alarms on your phone.

3. Schedule your to-dos on a calendar. This will declutter your brain and free you to create.

4. Set realistic yet challenging timeframes for your tasks.

5. Schedule similar tasks in the same timeframe.

6. Schedule your due dates on important tasks before the actual due dates. *This gives you some wiggle room and helps you be on time.*

7. Look into productivity apps and hacks. You may find an automated system that can handle some of your manual tasks.

8. If you juggle a lot of daily activities, identify short tasks you can do during the cracks in your schedule. Take it a step further—write the tasks on sticky notes, and when you have an opening, find a task, finish it, and throw that note in the trash.

9. It's hard to make smart decisions impulsively, so don't try. Schedule your decision-making.

10. After you schedule your tasks, stick to your schedule and *show up for it*!

Bonus! Learn to say no so you don't become too busy to fulfill your calling. If you don't take control of your calendar, it will take control of you. Use the next call to action to do this.

## Simple Prayer

Lord, teach me how to be proactive and
prioritize the right things. Amen.

## The Next Best Adventure Step

○ After you complete today's call to action, turn to chapter 27 to keep up
your momentum.

*After you schedule seven days of tasks,
check off day 26 as complete on the contents page.*

# Call to ACTION
## Micro Tasks and Due Dates

On day 25, you identified some actionable micro plans. Now let's prioritize them. From this point moving forward, schedule at least 15 minutes a day to do *something* related to your God-given dream. Take time right now to select and record some tasks for the next seven days. Then place those tasks on your calendar.

| Date | Micro Task |
|---|---|
|  |  |
|  |  |
|  |  |
|  |  |
|  |  |
|  |  |
|  |  |
|  |  |
|  |  |

# 27

# TAKE ACTION

*Take the first step in faith. You don't have to see
the whole staircase, just take the first step.*

DR. MARTIN LUTHER KING JR.

It takes action to see a dream come true. One remarkable dreamer who was also a doer understood this. You may have studied her in a history class—Joan of Arc. She was a peasant girl turned warrior who helped lead the French army to victory with wisdom and a fighting spirit. She could have made all the excuses in the book— she lacked military training and credentials. Yet Joan believed she was acting under divine guidance. One researcher writes that "Joan was granted command because of the religious society that believed anyone could receive a divine calling, and it should be listened to."[1] *Pretty remarkable, huh?*

After Moses stopped making excuses and started receiving his calling, God used him to lead more than half a million people out of Egypt. God instructed Moses to take the long route through the wilderness, away from enemy territory. God led the people with a pillar of cloud by day and with fire at night as they headed toward the Red Sea to the Promised Land. None of these adventures would have happened if Moses hadn't been willing to stop leading sheep and start leading Israel!

# Power Punch

Read this passage from Exodus 14:15-18 and underline all the action Moses took. Circle all the things God will do.

> The LORD said to Moses, "Why do you cry to me? Tell the people of Israel to go forward. Lift up your staff, and stretch out your hand over the sea and divide it, that the people of Israel may go through the sea on dry ground. And I will harden the hearts of the Egyptians so that they shall go in after them, and I will get glory over Pharaoh and all his host, his chariots, and his horsemen. And the Egyptians shall know that I am the LORD, when I have gotten glory over Pharaoh, his chariots, and his horsemen."

In our time together through this book, we won't be reading what happens after Moses begins to believe God's call on his life, but I highly urge you study your way through all of Exodus. There are plagues, the splitting of the Red Sea, and so many lessons learned as Moses responded in obedience. The vision God gave Moses at the burning bush became a reality. It commenced as Moses took steps of obedience, and it continued even after Moses's death.

What do you think would have happened if Moses had stood still or ignored God's voice? God probably would have chosen someone else. But influence follows obedience. Because Moses made a habit of saying yes, he became Israel's most important prophet and knew God face to face (Deuteronomy 34:10). He not only led the Israelites toward freedom but also received the Ten Commandments from God and knew Him intimately. Because Joan of Arc said yes, she not only led an army but also was canonized as a saint. (The only saintly thing about me is my holey jeans. Just kidding.)

Joan, Moses, you, me...we need to take that first step of saying yes. Why is that sometimes so hard? One reason is that we get distracted, comparing our calling with other people's or even trying to outdo them. Really? Let's remember that we're on the same team, working toward the same goal, and fighting a common enemy.

Each of us has a divine calling; we're smart in our own way but inspired by the same God. That's why it's imperative that we stay tethered to Him.

For 40 years, Moses led the Israelites. God kept His word and was *always* with him. Because you're a Christ-follower, the Holy Spirit lives in you and is with you (John 14:16-17). God is with you, helping you to align your will with His, empowering you to take action on His timeline, and moving through you in miraculous ways. God didn't create you to give up but to gain forward momentum, trusting Him in your call!

Let's make a habit of being in the Word, reminding ourselves of who God is while building confidence so we can move forward with courage into what God is doing today. Continue to be intentional and disciplined to do small, actionable tasks daily to get closer to your calling. And remember, we don't show up because the world needs more of *us*. We show up because people desperately need God, and He's inviting us and leading us into His redemptive story.

Take action and believe God is who He says He is. He called you to something significant because He's significant. Behind every dream that comes true are so many unseen acts of obedience from men and women who trusted a God who placed something of significance before them. The world sees a final product, a career advancement, or an adopted child who is safely bonding with their new family. The frustrated tears, hours of trial and error, or wrestling through the Word may not seem noteworthy. But with the right perspective, every action can be seen as an act of worship. Remain faithful and stick to the divine strategic plan in this season. God has given it to you for a reason. Even though others may not see all your action steps of obedience as this dream comes into fruition, God does. He sees your tears, hears your fears, and is with you.

You take action because God asked you to. As you do, you will influence others for Him, and your relationship with Him will grow. Let Him be God of your life. What an honor and privilege to be in this time of history and to respond to His call!

## Simple Prayer

Lord, teach me to take action when You ask. Amen.

# The Next Best Adventure Step

○ After you work through today's call to action, read chapter 28 to mark some moments. If you've already completed chapter 28, go to the next unread chapter.

*Don't forget to check off day 27 as complete on the contents page.*

## Call to ACTION
### Do Stuff

Put the pedal to the metal—it's time to do stuff! Devote at least 15 minutes to your scheduled tasks today. After completed, check them off that calendar or scribble them off your to-do list.

# 28

# MARK THE MOMENT

*God surpasses our dreams when we reach past our personal plans and agenda to grab the hand of Christ and walk the path he chose for us. He is obligated to keep us dissatisfied until we come to him and his plan for complete satisfaction.*

BETH MOORE

My son, Max, lost his first baby tooth, and you would have thought he got elected president or won a rap battle against Weird Al. My parents helped us celebrate the momentous occasion by buying a tooth-shaped cake. We decorated the house and had a small family party. I think we even made up a first-tooth song (that sounded suspiciously like the happy birthday song).

Was it over the top ridiculous? Perhaps. But was it also ridiculously right? *Yes!* Max's tooth fell out because he is growing, and we didn't want that fact to wiggle right by unnoticed.

It's great to observe special moments, like birthdays or the last day of college. What if we also valued spiritual moments—conversion, repentance, or even the everyday endurance we need to keep running the race? Marking these moments gives space for a pause and helps us recognize them as snapshots of our development, the hard work we've endured, God's faithfulness, and the miraculous things He's done. We shouldn't speed by our growth moments as if we were driving an Indy car. Instead, we should savor them like we do the view on a Sunday drive. We need to give ourselves time to take them in as refreshing, picturesque, and honk-the-horn holy.

## Rocks of Remembrance

There's a long biblical tradition of marking special moments, of pausing to perceive God's presence and action. After God called Joshua to take over the responsibility of leading the Israelites, the nation had to cross the Jordan River to get to the Promised Land. In Joshua 4:2-3 the Lord spoke:

> Take twelve men from the people, from each tribe a man, and command them, saying, "Take twelve stones from here out of the midst of the Jordan, from the very place where the priests' feet stood firmly, and bring them over with you and lay them down in the place where you lodge tonight."

They did as instructed. A person from each of the 12 tribes crossed the river and picked up a stone from the middle. Joshua set up the 12 stones to remind the people that God miraculously stopped the Jordan River from flowing. The rock pile became known as the monument at Gilgal.

The Hebrew name Gilgal means "circle of stones."

> Joshua said to them, "Pass on before the ark of the LORD your God into the midst of the Jordan, and take up each of you a stone upon his shoulder, according to the number of the tribes of the people of Israel, that this may be a sign among you. When your children ask in time to come, "What do those stones

> mean to you?" then you shall tell them that the waters of the Jordan were cut off before the ark of the covenant of the LORD. When it passed over the Jordan, the waters of the Jordan were cut off. So these stones shall be to the people of Israel a memorial forever (Joshua 4:5-7).

The monument at Gilgal became a marker of God's faithfulness, power, provision, and might. In Scripture, God seems to enjoy marking moments. He used a rainbow to mark a promise He made to Noah (Genesis 9:12-17), and in the New Testament, Jesus instituted what we now call Holy Communion as a remembrance of Him (Luke 22:19-20).

## Marking Present-Day Moments

When I walked into my friend's apartment, I noticed she had placed trinkets on her bookshelves and windowsills. When I began to look closer, she began sharing stories about the knickknacks. Each one represented a moment of growth, from the time a stranger said an encouraging word to an answered prayer for healing. As my friend marked each of these significant moments with a memento, she paused to acknowledge God's grace and goodness.

Sometimes we mark moments in our journals or in our celebrations, by lifting up prayer and praise or by sharing posts on social media. An elephant trinket could remind you of that trip overseas when God brought you into a relationship with Him. Perhaps you took a photo of the first time you headed to your computer programming internship. Years later, as we stumble upon these markers, we're able to reflect on God's faithfulness.

We're pressing pause to remember a significant moment when our hearts' desires became deeply interwoven with God's dreams for us. Worlds collided, and as heaven invaded earth, we witnessed restoration, wholeness, peace, love, opportunity, and abundance. In these moments, we pause, set up a marker, and worship as we acknowledge our Creator's hand at work.

As you pursue your calling, how might you mark a meaningful moment? Prayerfully work through the next call to action, and continue to practice remembrance as you move forward.

## Simple Prayer

Lord, may I understand You greater as I take time to mark the moments when You move. Amen.

## The Next Best Adventure Step

Work through today's call to action, and then take your next step...

- ○ Did you get here from chapter 12? Turn back to chapter 13 to pick up where you left off.

- ○ Read chapter 29 to "do it again."

*Don't forget to check off day 28 as complete on the contents page.*

## Call to ACTION
### Moment Marker Map

What significant God moments have you experienced while pursuing your dream? Write them out, and then decide how you'll mark each one as a moment of remembrance.

# 29

# REPEAT WITH RESILIENCE

*Success is not what you have done compared to what others have done. Success is what you have done compared to what you were supposed to do.*

TONY EVANS

> Now listen, you who say, "Today or tomorrow we will go to this or that city, spend a year there, carry on business and make money." Why, you do not even know what will happen tomorrow. What is your life? You are a mist that appears for a little while and then vanishes. Instead, you ought to say, "If it is the Lord's will, we will live and do this or that." As it is, you boast in your arrogant schemes. All such boasting is evil. If anyone, then, knows the good they ought to do and doesn't do it, it is sin for them (James 4:13-17 NIV).

I don't know who needs to know this, but...turn to page 143.

A survey conducted in 2019 through One Poll shows that the average person grows frustrated after waiting 16 seconds for a webpage to load or waiting 25 seconds for a traffic signal to change.[1] We live in a society that provides instant gratification with same-day deliveries, fast-food drive-throughs, and dopamine hits from "likes" on social media. Our attention span is shrinking, and we have a hard time acknowledging that sometimes slow and steady *does* win the race.

Oh, wouldn't it be easy if you just showed up the first day and your in-season dream was done? Here's the thing, dreamer—you are most likely playing the long game on this one. To continue pursuing your dream, you need a heavenly perspective and healthy dose of endurance. Patience still is a virtue you'll need if your dream is to come true.

The thing that separates the successful from the slothful is the long-game look. Most likely, this dream won't come to pass in a five-second dash to the finish. You need to lace up your stamina sneakers and prepare yourself for many days of repetitive tasks and weariness as you chip away at that *big* result. You can blame Adam and Eve for the challenging and sometimes dull work we do (Genesis 3:17-19).

Stay the course. Keep a healthy perspective. You get to do this for God's glory and the good of others. Don't keep pushing this away for another day. If God has called you to it, *do it*! Just as James wrote, "If anyone, then, knows the good they ought to do and doesn't do it, it is sin for them" (James 4:17 NIV).

Each day, celebrate every small win, see God working, and acknowledge the momentum building as you check off those micro tasks. Keep showing up, do, repeat...and see that dream come true!

After all, God's pace is often slower than ours. But look at the ordinary things in life: Flowers don't blossom from seeds overnight. The best bread dough needs to rise before being baked. You were knit together in your mother's womb, and look at all that growth since then!

Raw talent turns into skill as you repeatedly train and work through tasks. Just look at Michael Jordan's basketball success and legendary work ethic. After getting cut from the varsity team as a high school sophomore, he committed to working even harder. The following year he made the team, and he went on to play in college, won NBA championships, earned MVP tiles, and is celebrated as one of the greatest players in history. Even as an all-star, Jordan would continue practicing after his team finished. His coaches said he was one of the hardest workers they had ever seen. Jordan understood that "if you do the work you get rewarded. There are no shortcuts in life."[2]

We yearn for maturity and slam dunks even before taking our first steps. What God does beautifully, He does slowly. As Charles Spurgeon once said, "By perseverance the snail reached the ark." Instead of remaining stuck or weary after a one-day sprint, let's be the snail that steadily moves, tenaciously reaching the destination God has for us.

Hebrews 12:1-2 offers this encouragement:

> Let us also lay aside every weight, and sin which clings so closely, and let us run with endurance the race that is set before us, looking to Jesus, the founder and perfecter of our faith, who for the joy that was set before him endured the cross, despising the shame, and is seated at the right hand of the throne of God.

## Simple Prayer

Lord, develop my endurance and perspective to pursue this thing You've called me to. Amen.

## The Next Best Adventure Step

Work through the following call to action, and then take your next step...

○   Read chapter 30 to cue the confetti.

*Don't forget to check off day 29 as complete on the contents page.*

## Call to ACTION
### Repeat

Let's do it again, friend! Work through developing more micro tasks on page 125, and then check some tasks off your list today.

# 30

## CONFETTI TO THE FACE

*This job has been given to me to do. Therefore, it is a gift.*
*Therefore, it is a privilege. Therefore, it is an offering I may*
*make to God. Therefore, it is to be done gladly, if it is done*
*for Him. Here, not somewhere else, I may learn God's way.*
*In this job, not in some other, God looks for faithfulness.*

ELISABETH ELLIOT

Confetti cannons, twinkly lights, and glitter-filled jars are common in the Randle household. In fact, the other day a friend asked if it's normal for people to have confetti so readily available. I promptly responded by throwing some at her. We are one day away from you completing *Dream Come True*. Imagine me over here throwing confetti with you too!

Remember how Moses went to the king of Egypt and asked him to set the Israelites free? The king responded with a no. So God did what only He could do, and instead of throwing confetti at the Egyptians, He sent ten plagues. Plagues of frogs, blood water, lice, disease, darkness...and the death of the firstborn child. The Israelites, however, marked their doors with lamb's blood so the angel of death would pass right over. As God saw the blood, He delivered His children from harm (Exodus 7–12).

The Lord then instructed Moses and Aaron to celebrate. "This is a day you are to commemorate; for the generations to come you shall celebrate it as a festival to the LORD—a lasting ordinance" (Exodus 12:14 NIV). This became known as Passover, one of the most important holidays in Judaism.

Passover displays a biblical pattern of protection and salvation. When we believe, the atoning blood of a spotless sacrificed Lamb covers our sin and delivers us from death. The Old Testament prophesied His coming, and the New Testament confirms that Jesus is the Lamb of God (John 1:29). There is so much eternal significance in this image.

The Lord instructed Moses and Aaron to celebrate, and we get to enter into celebration too. Life is overflowing with abundance; we're wildly free because of the blood Christ shed on the cross for our sins. His death, resurrection, and ascension to heaven prove He is the Messiah. Even in our wilderness seasons, we are headed for our promised land because of our relationship with Him.

Making time to recognize God's eternal gift of salvation and the sanctification process that follows gives us a heavenly perspective that we can often miss. Are you celebrating the freedom from sin and bondage God has given you? Are you seeing how Christ is moving in your life? Are you getting bogged down making excuses, or are you pursuing that to-do list and strategic plan? Christ will always be enough and worthy of *all* our praise.

The apostle Paul wrote a letter to the brand-new Thessalonian Christians to encourage them in their faith. Let's read part of what he wrote.

> We urge you, brothers, admonish the idle, encourage the fainthearted, help the weak, be patient with them all. See that no one repays anyone evil for evil, but always seek to do good to one another and to everyone. Rejoice always,

> pray without ceasing, give thanks in all circumstances; for this is the will of God in Christ Jesus for you (1 Thessalonians 5:14-18).

# Power Punch

It isn't *really* about your dream; it's about you entering into God's dream. We can apply Paul's passage to your dream-building days as we celebrate Christ in these ways:

- advise people not to be lazy
- encourage those lacking courage
- support those with limited capacity
- make sure no one takes revenge on wrongdoings
- attempt to do good
- celebrate forever
- pray and petition without stopping
- give gratitude in every situation...

*for this is Christ's plan for you.*

"Rejoice" is a verb; it's not just a feeling or an appearance but an action you choose. It's choosing to express joy instead of whimsically feeling it. Life can be uncomfortable and circumstances can be chaotic, even for children of God. But your soul can be settled. You get to decide every day to celebrate and see Christ and His faithfulness. He's worthy of confetti-like praise, don't you think?

As Paul continued in his letter, "May the God of peace himself sanctify you completely, and may your whole spirit and soul and body be kept blameless at the

Your determination in life is remarkable. I applaud your commitment to tracking down these words. Use that same tenacity to keep showing up to reach your dream!

coming of our Lord Jesus Christ. He who calls you is faithful; he will surely do it" (1 Thessalonians 5:23-24).

## Simple Prayer

Lord, I give You all the praise for my freedom.
Thank You! Amen.

## The Next Best Adventure Step

Work through the call to action, and then take your next step...

○  It's your last stop! Turn the page and read chapter 31.

*Don't forget to check off day 30 as complete on the contents page.*

# *Call to* ACTION
## Celebrate Christ

As you continue to pursue the dream God has for you, don't let the dream overshadow the dream giver! Let's celebrate Christ today. You can do this in a whole bunch of ways! Here are some suggestions to get you started:

- Tell somebody your faith story, the ways God has forgiven you, or how you see Him working in your life.

- Study the Bible today and celebrate what you're learning about Christ's character.

- Make a gratitude list of all the ways you're thankful for God.

- Turn on worship music and have a praise party (confetti optional).

Have some fun celebrating! After you do, work through these questions:

- Reflect on how you celebrated Christ today.

- How can you maintain this perspective to continue celebrating and worshipping Him in the days to come?

# 31

# IMPACT THE WORLD

*If the whole world thinks you're amazing, but your family thinks you suck, then you probably do. You aren't understanding influence and God's mandate.*

MARK SCHILLING

*Congrats on making it through act 3, the section that led you to take action. Drop a text or phone call to your accountability partner, sharing with them that today is the last day of the book and that you're ready to continue pursuing the goals set before you.*

☐ Sent the text—it's a dream come true!          ☐ No thanks, I'm still lazy.

Now, if you completed your dream in the 31-day time frame, I'd like to challenge you to consider dreaming even *bigger*. This book equips you to recognize the dream, develop some new mindsets, and respond to God's calling. And remember, you will have lots of varied dreams and callings throughout your life, and they will all play significant roles in the way you glorify God.

As your relationship with Christ deepens, you understand more about the dream He has for you right now. Knowing and following Him gives you a firm foundation and then sets you in motion toward the work God is inviting you to do. This is not "envisioning your dream until it turns into reality." Instead, this is allowing Christ to reveal His dream for you.

We're often afraid to dream big. We keep our God-given voice to ourselves because we're too concerned about what others may say. We become sloth-like on mission—or realize we were never on mission at all. We laid idle. Barren. Displaying no fruit as the world spins around us worshipping idols in all the wrong places.

The American dream often includes a high-paying job, fancy car, or mansion. I get it. As a child, I was desperate for that Barbie dream house. Now, as I pursue the Christ-centered dream, I see that my longing isn't for a physical object. God's dream houses everything I could ever need—Himself.

We have watched Moses at the burning bush as he transitioned from making excuses to pursuing his calling and finding freedom. As you continue to read the book of Exodus, you see Moses's dependence on God. He experiences many miracles and a deeper connection with God as he helped free the Israelites from captivity.

## God Is for You

The same God, the one who redeems and restores, uses all your excuses to point you back to Him. He is with you and calling you to a new level of influence for Him. Wherever God is leading is where you need to be.

We're all influencers and leaders in different ways. Our dreams may lead us to creative positions where God uses us to make an impact for Him. Why don't you take a few minutes to brainstorm the influential places you've been over the past few years? As I've pursued various dreams God had for me, He's created opportunities to prophesy to Hollywood producers, pray for healing in the slums of Africa, teach kindergarteners at vacation Bible school (whoops, I made a kid cry), and aggressively yell "I have an Emmy®!" while high-fiving a literary agent. (I'm still embarrassed about that, but hey, you're holding this book, aren't you?)

But the most important and influential place I've been is in my home and with those who I look in the eye daily—immediate family, church family, coworkers, neighbors. The greatest desire of my heart isn't to write a bestseller or speak to huge audiences. My biggest dream is to help my kids love and worship Jesus with passion and integrity while teaching them how to manage their gifts well. I want to serve my local church and to see our island community and friendships flourish for the Lord.

Do you think it's possible to invest in those right in front of you while pursuing your dream come true? I'm a work in progress, but I think the answer is yes. I may have classified myself as the world's worst cook, but you better believe I can bring the new parents from our church some dinner from our favorite taco shop. As a working mom, I may not have time to join the PTA, but I'll coach my daughter's soccer team on the weekend. Figure out what works for you and continue to show up. Let's be dreamers who prioritize living present and loving local.

I'm sure you know how to give love, but can you remember the times you've been the recipient of loving impact too? A few weeks ago, I was in my home office crying and feeling overwhelmed as my husband and I struggled through a decision we had to make at our creative agency. My friend Amy wasn't aware of our business decisions, but God inspired her to reach out at just the right time. *Knock, knock, knock.* There stood a vase of sunflowers—my favorite—and a sweet card of encouragement signed by Amy. This moment was really special, and I felt seen by a God who loves me so much He'd speak to a sweet, action-taking friend on my behalf.

What I appreciated most about the situation is that Amy and I had never frolicked in a field of sunflowers, raving about them as our favorites. She just made a mental note during casual conversations that sunflowers are special to me. She saw me, and because she did, I saw God.

As we *truly* see the people standing right in front of us and continue getting to know God's voice, our impact grows. Oftentimes our callings and dreams aren't about the final destination but the travelers we see along the journey. It's an honor to be invited to share others' hurt, struggle, success, and celebrations and to watch God move in it all. When we take time to recognize the sacred ground on which we stand, God increases our influence, and others are blessed. We are too!

## God Is with You

How did you become influential? It was not by striving but by seeking Christ. As your intimacy with Him deepens, you learn how to influence others for Him. We're driven not by worldly definitions of success but by Christ's mandate. I've said it a few times, but I want our last chapter to shout this from the rooftops: Throughout the seasons of your life, God is designing many dreams for you that will bring Him glory and benefit others.

> You are the salt of the earth, but if salt has lost its taste, how shall its saltiness be restored? It is no longer good for anything except to be thrown out and trampled under people's feet.
>
> You are the light of the world. A city set on a hill cannot be hidden. Nor do people light a lamp and put it under a basket, but on a stand, and it gives light to all in the house. In the same way, let your light shine before others, so that they may see your good works and give glory to your Father who is in heaven (Matthew 5:13-16).

A stagnant faith results in stunted growth. Commit to consistently pursuing Christ as He pursues you. As you mature and walk in obedience, your dreams grow bigger, your childlike wonder awakens, and your calling is confirmed. Remember, you aren't alone in this. God is with you—guiding, leading, and casting vision over the things He's placed before you.

Perhaps you have experienced seasons of restlessness, or you've struggled to communicate freely. This is the season your voice, gifts, and talents find their full expression in God's dream for you. You answered the call, and you know above all that He is the hero of the story. God is living out His story in your life, and that is the driving factor that empowers you to show up in this wild adventure.

God is placing you with people who need breakthroughs and solutions. They need to feel loved and valued. They need to be shown kindness and to be covered in prayer. When Jesus told His disciples, "Let your light shine before others, so that they may see your good works and give glory to your Father who is in heaven" (Matthew 5:16), He was talking to us too.

Light is a common biblical metaphor for truth, knowledge, freedom, salvation, goodness, holiness, and godly character. Just as a solar-powered flashlight needs the sun in order to shine, so do you...but I'm not talking about catching rays at the beach. I'm talking about Jesus, the light source that fills you to overflowing. Jesus said, "I am the light of the world. Whoever follows me will not walk in darkness, but will have the light of life" (John 8:12).

On the next page is your final call to action. Think about the people you're influencing. Today I'm cheering for you, your dream, and the people you are called to reach. I'm also cheering for your future dreams that are being shaped by your faithfulness today! Because whether it's in this dream or the next, God is on the move. Not primarily because you are pursuing your dream but because He's pursuing you. Happy dreaming, friend—God has some great plans for you. As you step out to act, He is making His dream come true!

## Simple Prayer

Lord, may Your influence in my life empower me
to encourage others for Your glory. Amen.

## The Next Best Adventure Step

○ You did it! You're all done. The next best step is to work through today's call to action and then to check out the bonus content or continue to pursue the steps God is designing for you!

*Don't forget to check off day 31 as complete on the contents page.*

# Call to ACTION
## Let It Shine

Who is God inviting you to influence right now? List their names and reflect on the ways God is shining through you. If this is a struggle for you, prayerfully ask God ways that you are reflecting Him and can reflect Him even more. Spend some time thanking God for developing godly character in you!

**God is inviting me to influence...**        **He is shining through me by...**

_____        _____

_____        _____

_____        _____

_____        _____

_____        _____

_____        _____

_____        _____

_____        _____

_____        _____

Bonus

# 32

# NO, I CAN'T DO IT

Have *you* decided now might not be the best time to step into that thing you feel called to do? Trust me; I get it. I decided that too for ten years. No matter how many pep-talks I gave myself, I couldn't change my mind and heart—only God could do that. He had to overcome the power of comfort, procrastination, selfish ambition, comparison, and doubt that paralyzed me.

Recently I saw this quote from a well-known person in the faith:

> God has already done everything He's going to do. If you want success, if you want wisdom, if you want to be prosperous and healthy, you're going to have to do more than meditate and believe; you must boldly declare words of faith and victory over yourself and your family.[1]

Positive self-talk is great, but this quote feels manipulative, like so much feel-good fluff. As if by chanting this loud enough and often enough, I'll get what I always wanted. It's genie-in-a-bottle theology. You know what's missing from that quote? *God!* Let me rewrite it for us: If you want success, spend time with God. Period. End of sentence.

If you do some soul searching and discover that you're saying no to the things God has invited you to, I wonder...do you like to feel in control? I mean, who doesn't, right? But are you treating God like an accessory rather than your first priority? Are you inviting Him over to your house when you find time in your schedule? Well, friend, God invited you to *His planet*. Like any great host will do, He's asking you to join Him at the table. But of course, instead of sitting, you'll probably choose to kneel at His footstool because His presence is powerful.

God is sovereign and good. He won't demand things of you or wave fairy dust on your head to turn you into a robotic doer. He doesn't schedule six-month dream reviews. God wants to take you by the hand and lead you every step of the way. His dreams are far greater than your eye can see anyway. He selected you to be a character in His story, and He's leading the journey. Isn't it amazing that you get to be part of His adventurous plan?

## *Call to* ACTION
### Things to Prayerfully Consider

If you've glimpsed God's dream for you, but you're flat-out saying, "No, I can't do it," I'd like to challenge you with a few questions that have helped me find freedom.

- Do you truly think your dream is from God?

- Are you typically a dreamer and idea person? Or a realistic get-it-done person? Do you see your personality type hindering any forward momentum?

- If your dream seems overwhelming, what are practical ways you can focus on Christ more than you focus on your dream?

- The apostle Paul was a tentmaker while he shared the gospel with others. How might your dream fit in the context of your everyday life?

- Are you feeling overwhelmed or underwhelmed because the dream seems too big or too small? How do you measure success?

- Imagine seeing someone else four months from now taking steps toward this dream. How would you feel?

- How are you cultivating your relationship with God? Are you practicing spiritual disciplines, like studying the Word, praying, and attending a local church?

As you spend time in God's presence, He can bring healing in the areas that might be causing you to defer your dream. Let Him give you a collaborative spirit so you can honor God and His dream for you. Can you choose to reject it? Yes. But that's boring. Also, does that course of action lead you to God's best for your life?

# 33

# I FEEL VISIONLESS

Do you feel like you don't have a dream or vision to steward in this season? This bonus chapter is for you. I'd like to challenge you to consider this thought: If you feel visionless, that doesn't mean you lack vision. It means you need to look through a different lens. Don't let the famous verse in Proverbs apply to you: "Where there is no vision, the people perish" (Proverbs 29:18 KJV).

 The Message paraphrases Proverbs 29:18, "If people can't see what God is doing, they stumble all over themselves; but when they attend to what he reveals, they are most blessed."

As my kids and I read the great children's novel *Charlotte's Web*, the story spoke to me about the dreams we're stewarding. Funny how God can use anything to bring us a more in-depth perspective, huh? Here's the CliffsNotes version: A farmer wants to kill a piglet because it was the runt of the litter. But the farmer's daughter rescues the piglet and names him Wilbur. Wilbur, searching for friends, notices Charlotte, a special spider that other animals ignore. Together, they have some pretty amazing adventures.

Are you tempted to kill a runt of a dream that God is trying to save? If you rescued that little dream, could it hold value for others? All dreams are important—small, big, and in between.

Look through the lens of faith to see what God is doing. He is likely giving you more dreams than you realize. Helping to mentor that college student, sharing a meal with your neighbor, developing a new system at work...these are just as important as the grandiose dreams that scare the poop out of you. You know why? Because God is placing you there.

## *Call to* ACTION
### Two Questions and a Prayer

- How am I comparing myself to others? Is this giving me a healthy perspective of my situation?

- What do my day-to-day activities include?

- "God, will You help me see what You are doing in my daily life? Do you have dreams for me that I'm not seeing or that I have discounted?"

Still feel like you lack vision? How can you seek to better understand God's character and the truth of His Word? Are you spending time in Scripture every day? Learning more about Him and His big-picture story will help you understand who He's created you to be. Vision develops as you understand the Author's world and your place in it.

# 34

# DO I HAVE TO HUSTLE?

No. You don't have to hustle to prove this dream worthwhile, but you *do* need a sense of what God is doing. Your work ethic can't make a dream holy; God does. Managing your God-goals well requires you to hear His voice and pursue whatever He's asking you to do. One day it may be taking the kids to the beach; another it may be working until 2:00 a.m. to launch a new website.

To achieve something that once felt unachievable, you have to show up for it, whittling away little by little until it's complete. And you can maintain a healthy work/life balance in the process. God empowers us to maintain momentum so the dream can blossom. You will never have to outrun the pace of God's grace. Just keep steady with Him, and the power and grace to press on will happen—without the life-sucking hustle. We get to rest in Christ while representing Him.

## *Call to* ACTION
### Am I facing hustle fatigue?

As I studied a healthy work/life balance, I learned a few key things. Hustle and holy can coincide, but hustle fatigue (I made up that phrase) is what happens when hustling starts to hurt. Here's what I mean.

- Are you feeling sick, anxious, or exhausted?
- Are you lashing out in unusual ways?

- Do the simplest tasks leave you feeling overwhelmed?
- Are you looking for affirmation in unhealthy ways?
- Do you feel like a failure?
- Are you overindulging in tacos, TV, naps, alcohol...?
- Do you feel alone?
- Do you lack motivation?

I'm not a counselor or doctor, but based on my experience, if you answered yes to a few of these questions, you may be facing burnout and overwhelm. Your hustle got harmful.

There is a big difference between butterflies and burnout as you pursue your dream. Butterflies are often simply caused by nerves, but burnout is more likely the result of a lack of boundaries. You may have butterflies as you work toward your God-given dream, but you shouldn't launch any dreams when you're experiencing hustle fatigue.

Consider ways you can scale back and enjoy a full day of Sabbath rest at least once a week. Do the things that create space to recognize God, things that make you feel alive. Read your Bible, worship, pray, go on a hike, drink coffee with your friend, slowly walk the aisles of Target, play games with the kids, or read that fiction book on your hammock.

Prayerfully consider how to chase your dream and maintain a balanced life, and be intentional about maintaining that as a high priority! You can honor God by honoring His boundaries for you. If you continue to struggle with this, consider talking to a trusted friend, counselor, medical professional, or church leader.

# 35

## IS THIS A SELFISH DREAM?

It's hard to know if you should pursue your dream with passion and persistence, because it could be the wrong dream altogether.

### Call to ACTION
#### Is My Dream Selfish?

Identify one of your dreams and then answer these true/false questions. Yes, the "correct" answers are blatantly obvious, but I hope they stimulate your thinking.

|  | True | False |
|---|---|---|
| 1. I think about the process of my dream as much as I think about the result. | ☐ | ☐ |
| 2. I believe I can accomplish anything with enough effort. | ☐ | ☐ |
| 3. If I fail, I'm still secure. | ☐ | ☐ |
| 4. My only incentive for showing up is monetary gain. | ☐ | ☐ |
| 5. I can't create my destiny. | ☐ | ☐ |
| 6. I will begin to understand my self-worth as this dream falls into place. | ☐ | ☐ |
| 7. I need help working toward my dream, and I can ask for it. | ☐ | ☐ |

|  | True | False |
|---|---|---|
| 8. The main reason I have this dream is to make me happy. | ☐ | ☐ |
| 9. I fail sometimes, and that's okay. | ☐ | ☐ |
| 10. Completing my dream will give me total fulfillment. | ☐ | ☐ |
| 11. My relationship with God is the most important facet of my life. | ☐ | ☐ |
| 12. I will reach success when I become the best in my field. | ☐ | ☐ |
| 13. My romantic relationships and hobbies are not the keys to my happiness. | ☐ | ☐ |
| 14. I will do whatever it takes to pursue that thing, even if it means I have to act weasely. | ☐ | ☐ |
| 15. My vision board doesn't feel man-made but God-ordained. | ☐ | ☐ |
| 16. I ignore my responsibilities to pursue this dream. | ☐ | ☐ |

## Calculate Your Score

Put an X by each odd-numbered question you answered "false." Put an X by each even-numbered question you answered "true." If you marked some questions, your dream may be based on your own ambitions or desires, and that dream is likely to glorify *you*! Ask yourself,

- Who is the focus of my dream?
- What motivates me to pursue this dream?

God desires you to dream, but He wants to be your foundation. There are healthy and unhealthy ways to pursue a dream. I'd like to challenge you to keep a healthy and godly perspective on the things God has for you. Your dream shouldn't be centered on you but on Christ and His will for your life.

So if you marked any of the questions, perhaps you can conclude that your dream seems selfish. Here's the greatest thing about God though. When we repent, He quickly forgives our selfish motives. He transforms our destructive desires into productive reminders to turn our gaze to Him.

Prayerfully ask God for some healthy next steps. Invite Him to be the center of your life!

# 36

# I'M POWERFUL AND ENOUGH

Have you ever heard someone say something like this? "I envisioned my dream coming true, so it did." Maybe that person wrote down their goal every day, and *poof!* there was that six-figure salary or the McDreamy husband or a partridge in a pear tree.

Was it luck? Did God bless her dream? Did she work hard because her focus was on that one thing? We can't know for sure, but what I do know is that the thought feels incomplete to me.

Yes, we work hard, set goals, have positive self-talk, and embrace God-given dreams. That much is biblical. But imagining something to be true doesn't make it so.

We are finite creatures, and our limitations are real. So are our circumstances. I recently met some children living in extreme poverty in a small village overseas. They were beautiful and resilient, and their courage was inspiring. But no matter how much they envisioned healthy meals, comfortable homes, and safe surroundings, they couldn't dream those things into existence.

Wishful thinking is just that, a wish. We. Need. A. Savior.

We can celebrate that we are en route to redemption and full restoration, but let's not make this all about us. Yes, you're loved. Yes, you're enough. Yes, you're powerful. But that's not the end of the story. Or even the most important part.

The self-help gospel points to you, but the gospel of Christ points to Him. The self-help sermon says, "Look at you perform!" The Christ-centered sermon says, "Look at the One who paid the price for your sin." Christianity isn't about performance. You don't have to strive to prove your worth. Instead, you get to worship the One who is worthy.

We're loved so much that God gave His one and only Son to fix humanity's brokenness. The moment Christ came into your life, Holy Spirit began living in you and ministering through you. From this place of transparency, transformation and change happen. We don't produce hope or healing; Jesus does.

As the kids in the poverty-ridden village dreamed and prayed for safety, Christ gave others a dream that empowered and equipped them to fill that great need. He gave people vision and finances to set up self-sustaining farms that would bring these families a better future. God is putting dreams on your heart to bless many others. The key isn't how powerful you are; it's knowing the powerful solution we have in Christ.

# CLOSING CREDITS

God—Your sustaining hand was on my life before I even recognized You. I'm constantly amazed by Your ability to create something out of what seems like nothing. All the praise hands for that!

Matt, Max, and Zoey—you three are the most significant dreams come true in my life. I'm proud of you and the work God is entrusting to you.

Dad, Mom, Cathy, and John—the Marsella gang is not complete without cheering one another on. Thank you for being a fam of dreamers who get stuff done. Love you lots.

Brayden Brookshier—Your love for God's Word is contagious! Thank you for working on this book. What a dream come true to see you and Ariana become parents during this process.

Gene Skinner—you are a man of grace, wisdom, and kindness. I'm so thankful for all the effort you pour out into our books. You make me a better writer and communicator.

Barb Sherrill—thank you for giving me space to create and for believing in this message.

To the rest of the Harvest House team—thank you for using your God-given gifts and talents daily. The world is a lot brighter (and wordier) because of you!

Steve Laube—you saw my potential and spoke strength into my purpose. Thank you.

Malinda Just—thank you for providing biblical research for this book. I know your book-writing dreams are well on their way to coming true, and I'm cheering you on!

The Schillings, the Bellars, my church family (past and present), our Freedom Creatives prayer team, Michelle Cuthrell, Candace Payne, and Brynn Shamp—your prayers, support, friendship, and leadership in my life are so valued and appreciated. Thank you for always encouraging me to keep dreaming.

To you, dear reader—thank you for investing your time and talents into reading these pages. Look at what God did!

# NOTES

## CHAPTER 18: HELLO DREAM, I SEE YOU

1. Mark Murphy, "Neuroscience Explains Why You Need to Write Down Your Goals If You Actually Want to Achieve Them," *Forbes*, April 15, 2018, https://www.forbes.com/sites/markmurphy/2018/04/15/neuroscience-explains-why-you-need-to-write-down-your-goals-if-you-actually-want-to-achieve-them/.

## CHAPTER 19: THE RIGHT SEASON

1. "Apostle Paul's Timeline—Study Resources," Blue Letter Bible, https://www.blueletterbible.org/study/paul/timeline.cfm.
2. Jenny Randle, *Getting to Know God's Voice: Discover the Holy Spirit in Your Everyday Life* (Eugene, OR: Harvest House, 2020), 13.

## CHAPTER 20: KNOW YOUR ~~WHY~~ WHO

1. Simon Sinek, "How Great Leaders Inspire Action," TED, September 2009, https://www.ted.com/talks/simon_sinek_how_great_leaders_inspire_action.

## CHAPTER 23: THE TALENTED AND GIFTED PROGRAM

1. J.W. Lo, "Grace," in *Lexham Theological Wordbook*, ed: D. Mangum, D.R. Brown, R. Klippenstein, and R. Hurst (Bellingham, WA: Lexham Press, 2014).

## CHAPTER 27: TAKE ACTION

1. Frances White, "8 Joan of Arc Myths Busted," *All About History*, May 2, 2019, https://www.historyanswers.co.uk/history-of-war/8-joan-of-arc-myths-busted/.

## CHAPTER 29: REPEAT WITH RESILIENCE

1. John Anderer, "Hurry Up! Modern Patience Thresholds Lower Than Ever Before, Survey Finds," *Study Finds*, September 3, 2019, www.studyfinds.org/hurry-up-modern-patience-thresholds-lower-than-ever-before-survey-finds/.
2. Hannah Hutyra, "102 Michael Jordan Quotes That Show Strength and Dedication," *KeepInspiring.me*, March 24, 2020, https://www.keepinspiring.me/michael-jordan-quotes/.

## CHAPTER 32: NO, I CAN'T DO IT

1. Joel Osteen, *Your Best Life Now*, rev. ed. (New York, NY: FaithWords, 2015), 132.

# ABOUT THE AUTHOR

*Jenny Randle* is an Emmy®-award winning video editor who went on a journey to discover what it really means to live on purpose. From enjoying a career in the heart of Hollywood editing for billion-dollar franchises to becoming a faith-based leader and chart-topping podcaster, Jenny's voice and work has been featured in hundreds of notable films and print and media outlets.

Her search for meaning in the everyday moments of life has led her to start a ministry organization, write numerous books, and speak at major conferences, women's retreats, and churches nationally. Jenny speaks on topics ranging from understanding the Holy Spirit to empowering God-given creativity with authenticity, humor, and biblical authority. She guides others into freedom in their personal lives and leadership environments as they discover how God designed them to dream for Him.

In early 2018, Jenny and her husband, Matt, formed Freedom Creatives, a parachurch ministry dedicated to developing resources that merge profound gospel-centered truths with practical application. Freedom Creatives provides courses, coaching, and in-person and online events that champion people into their calling for Christ.

Jenny and Matt live on an island in Northern Florida with their two kids, Max and Zoey. They enjoy beach life and pray they'll continue to throw confetti-like praise in the air for all their days. For more information or to invite Jenny to speak at your event, visit jennyrandle.com.

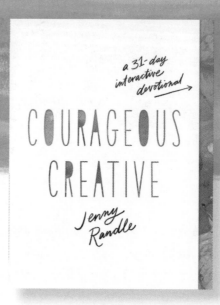

You've courageously pursued that dream come true
and the adventures God has for you. Now...

## Stretch Your God-Given Creativity

Do you need some pep in your creative step? *Courageous Creative* is written for you. In this hands-on journey, you will...

- Find the tools and encouragement you need to discover your God-given identity and express your thoughts
- Cultivate your creativity with 31 days of creative challenges
- Experience creative breakthrough and spiritual freedom

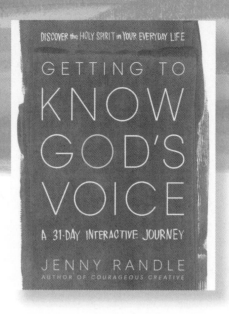

DISCOVER the HOLY SPIRIT in YOUR EVERYDAY LIFE

# GETTING TO KNOW GOD'S VOICE

A 31-DAY INTERACTIVE JOURNEY

JENNY RANDLE
AUTHOR OF COURAGEOUS CREATIVE

## Ditch the Distractions and Dismantle Doubt

Understand the ways God can speak into your personal life as Jenny comes alongside you and equips you to...

- Navigate nine common hang-ups in hearing the Holy Spirit
- Amplify the sound of God's voice in your life with 31 practical "Hearing Aids"
- Overflow with purpose as you respond to God's voice